# TELLING
# TEDDY

## J D Stockholm

J D STOCKHOLM

**Other Works.**

Dear Teddy

Dark Ramblings of the Phoenix

ISBN-13: 978-1478295419

ISBN-10: 1478295414

## TELLING TEDDY

Mr. Ted holds the hand of his six-year-old friend as they share more of his deepest secrets. Poignant and bold, the boy's courageous words are detailed and real. He takes you farther into his abusive life and broken mind as he survives the tangled deceit and lies of his everydays. Sit alongside him. Hear his voice and listen with your heart as he opens it up once more.

His story continues…

Based on a true story. Though names, places and dates may have been changed.

Feel free to contact me.

Contact

dearmrted@gmail.com

http://jdstockholm.com/

http://www.facebook.com/dearmrted

# J D STOCKHOLM

## ONE

*Mr. Ted. I love you very much.*

I love my Mr. Ted. He is all mine and he is magic. He keeps me safe from the bad man. I hug him all tight. We sit on the floor by the fire. I don't be allowed to sit on the chairs. I am too evil.

Me and Mr. Ted like to write stories. He tells me what to write. Then I draw the pictures about it and we make it all nice. I put it in my scrap book. My Nan bought me the scrap book. It is big and has lots of pages. It has a car on the front and my name.

I write about all my stories inside it. I don't write about the bad man though. I don't tell anyone about the bad man. He can hear me. He reads minds. Mr. Ted keeps him away.

My mum says she doesn't want to hear about it. But the bad man makes me scared in my tummy. Mr. Ted says don't tell anyone. If I do then the bad man will come and get me. My mum says he's a demon. He is from the devil like me. But I'm not a demon. I'm just evil. But my mum is going to make me all better. She gives me medicine.

The medicine doesn't get to work yet. That's why the bad man comes at night. Then he does the hurt thing. It makes me scared. Mr. Ted says it's a secret. The bad man bites me and scratches me. Then I don't get away. My mum doesn't hear me shout. The bad man makes me go to sleep.

Me and Mr. Ted write a story about a penguin and a mouse. I make all the pictures. They live together in the mouse house. They are very happy. They go to the fair and have candy floss. The mouse is very kind. He shares all his things with the penguin. He shares his candy floss. The penguin thinks it is very yummy.

Me and my Nan are going to the fair. It is my birthday and I get to be six. My mum and dad don't come. They have lots of things to do at home.

I get candy floss. But I don't get to give Mr. Ted any of it. My Nan says it will make his fur all sticky. Then my mum will be mad and he will have to go in the rubbish bin. He is my Mr. Ted. I didn't want him to go away in the rubbish bin.

## TELLING TEDDY

No candy floss for Mr. Ted. I tell him no. He doesn't be sad about it. He is a good Mr. Ted.

I am allowed to go on the rides. They make it all tickle inside. My Nan goes on them too. She likes the rides. I hold onto my Nan's hand. We get on rides that are like tea cups. We sit in the cup and it spins around in circles. It makes me all dizzy in my head. My Nan says I am being silly because it makes my tongue fall out of my mouth and my eyes go across.

There are big rides too. They go very fast and I want to go on them. I ask my Nan but she says I am too small.

I am big.

I am six.

My Nan says, "Not big enough."

I pull a sulky face and make my arms fold up. But she says I'm still too small. One day I will be big. Then I will go on them. There is a board with a line on it. I stand on my tip toes. My Nan says I am cheating.

We finish on all the rides and we ride on a tram. It is time to go home again. My Nan takes me to my house. My mum and dad are there. They don't remember it is my birthday. But I am not allowed them anyway until I don't be evil anymore. My mum says when I am better I can have one like my brother does. I try my best to get better. I take all my medicine.

I sit by the fire with Mr. Ted after my Nan goes home. We draw a picture about the candy floss and the tea cup rides. My mum is in the kitchen. She is cooking dinner. It is roast chicken. My dad sits at the table and drinks his beer in the can. He asks me what I am doing. I tell him I am drawing a picture about the fair.

"Can I look at it?"

I show him my book. He gets the pictures in his big hands. He asks me if I drew them myself. I make my head all nod. "Yes I did." They are mine.

My dad does the stare thing. "It's bad to tell lies."

But I don't be lying. I did them myself. I didn't trace them. Me and Mr. Ted made them. I get my paper and my pencil. I show my dad how to draw the rides and the penguin. He picks it up. He says it is very good.

My dad asks if he can look at my story. I show him the one about the fair. My dad sits on the floor with me and then he looks at my book. He reads it out loud. He makes a silly voices with it. It makes me laugh. He makes the voices sound all funny.

He gets my hand. He puts it inside his pants. I wish I got to hug Mr. Ted. My dad gets to the end of the page. He tells me to turn it to the next one. He says my stories are very good. He wants to read some more. He keeps my hand in his pants until it get all wet. He tells me to go and wash my hands. It is nearly dinner time.

## TWO

*Mr. Ted. I didn't eat all my dinner. I didn't mean to. I did the bad thing with my dad. I feel bad inside.*

Fork on the left. Knife on the right.

I write with my right hand. That's what Mr. Ted says. The knife goes in my right hand.

Then I get the paper towel. I fold it all neat and special. Like my mum says I have to.

"I don't want some screwed up piece of crap on my table. We're not too poor that we have to look it."

I put the spoon on the paper towel. But it has to face the right way. I make it face the right way. All in a straight line and nice and neat. Like my mum said.

One. Two. Three. Knife. Fork. Spoon. Not the paper towel. Paper towel makes me say four. Four is bad. It makes the bad man come and get me. I don't ever say four.

We eat dinner at the big table. I don't be allowed to start until my dad says yes. My dad doesn't say yes all the time. Not when I am bad. Sometimes I am too bad. Then he says no.

"If you can't behave like a normal child then why should I feed you?"

No dinner when I am bad. I am bad lots of times. The evil inside makes me do it. I don't want to be bad.

We sit at the table. I don't be able to see my mum's head because there is big giant flowers on the table. I only get to see my brother and my dad.

My brother gets eggs to eat. He doesn't like to eat the chicken. He doesn't like any food ever. My mum says because the hospital made him all scared of it. They got a tube and put it down his neck so he didn't die when he came out of her tummy.

I wish I didn't get any chicken. It's nice. But my food is all the way in my feet and in my legs. It's nearly at the top. Then it will come out of my neck and make me get the sick out. I don't want to get the sick out. Then my mum and dad will be mad. I'm not hungry.

I got peas and green things on my plate. My dad says they are beans. But beans are orange and they have sauce. They don't be green. Jack got beans for a beanstalk. They were white. He didn't get green beans too. Beans aren't long.

My Nan says when you eat peas and beans they make your bottom trumpy.

"What's wrong with your food?" My dad asks me.

I tell him I am all filled up. Right to the top. From my boots to my neck. My dad tells me to stop being stupid. He doesn't care if I am all filled up to the damn ceiling. He paid for the food. I better eat it or else. There was people that live in dumps and don't get food.

In my story book. There was a travel man. He didn't have a house. He got to live in the forest. Not the dumps. He had a bag on a stick. He was hungry and he just had a pan and a stone and a fire. He asked the people if they could give him things to put in the pan. They did because they were all nice. He made some soup. Everyone got to eat it. It was very nice.

My dad bangs his hand on the table. He makes me jump. My tummy jumps in circles inside and it tickles. My tummy does a roly-poly thing.

"Wake up."

My dad finishes all his dinner, then he goes to his shed. He likes to be in there. He has his bikes inside. He is making a new motorbike. It will be big and giant. When I got big my dad said I could have a ride.

My mum takes my plate away. She wants to wash up. She doesn't want to wait for me to be slow and mess around. There isn't anything else to eat if I get hungry later.

Me and Mr. Ted lie on the floor by the fire. We like to read. My eyes are sleepy. They go to sleep and I don't know about it. Mr. Ted goes to sleep too. Then he doesn't wake up to tell me my dad is coming.

My dad is mad.

He makes me stand up. My eyes are still sleeping. My head is dizzy. Like I have been spinning around and around. Like a merry-go-round. My Nan says I make my head shake when I do that. Maybe it would spin right off and roll away.

My brain is all fast asleep. I don't say anything to my dad. He smacks his hand across my face. I don't be able to stand up. I fall over but the chair is there and I don't land on the floor.

## TELLING TEDDY

My dad pulls me to the table. He makes me sit on the chair. He squishes my shoulders all down. It hurts. I try to get away. But he has big hands. They squeeze all tight and I can't move. He has my plate.

"Eat it."

I don't want to. I'm all bad inside. It makes me all filled up. My dad puts the fork in my hand. He squeezes my fingers all together. I put the food in my mouth. It's all bad and cold. I squeeze my face all up.

My dad sits in the big chair. He moves the flowers. He looks at me all the time. I don't like it when he does that. Sometimes he smacks me when he does the stare thing.

My plate gets all empty.

"Upstairs," my dad says.

I don't move. It doesn't be time for bed yet. I don't want the bad man to get me. I didn't eat my dinner. I was all bad. My dad smacks the table. My plate jumps in the air. It all makes a loud noise.

My dad gets up. He comes to me. Then he smacks me. My ears hurt inside. It makes me cry. He gets my arm and pulls me off the chair. Then he takes me upstairs.

We go all the way up the stairs very fast. He takes me to the bedroom. Then he pushes me in and I fall over.

"Do not make a sound."

He closes the door and locks it. I don't have Mr. Ted. I forgot him. He is downstairs. Maybe the bad man is hiding. I look under the bed. He isn't there. I crawl to the window. I stay there all night. I look at the door when my mum and dad come bed. They turn off the light. I don't want the bad man to come.

## THREE

*Mr. Ted. I'm so stupid. My Mummy is right. I just be bad all the time. Please make me be better.*

I stand in the kitchen. I wait for my medicine then I have to go to school. My mum is making it for me in my cow cup. The one with the cow picture all cleaned off. She gives it me on a big metal spoon. It's all hot in my mouth and my eyes want to run. I don't make it go all the way down to my feet. The sick in my tummy wants to come out very fast. I get to the rubbish bin and put my head all the way in it. It smells yucky inside.

I let the sick get out and it doesn't get on my shoes. Then my mum doesn't get mad because I don't make a mess.

One sick.

Two sick.

I don't like two, but it is okay. Mr. Ted says that two isn't very bad. It hurts my tummy all inside and I can't get more sick out to make it three. It makes my eyes want to cry. I don't let my mum see. She gets mad if I cry. I don't want to be a big cry baby.

My mum gives me a jumping bean too. She made it herself when I was getting the sick out. It's red and white. It isn't very good. It doesn't jump, not like the ones that my Nan buy'd for me.

I don't like the jumping beans. My mum says they are medicine too. They will help to get the badness away. She asks me what the devil says. I tell her about the bad things I like to do. She says I have to swallow them. They make me go to the toilet lots of times. My mum doesn't let me use the toilet lots of times outside. She says I have to go upstairs. I don't like it up there. The bad man is hiding.

I make it roll about in my hand. My mum tells me to stop it.

"Can't you just do as you're told?"

I keep it in my hand. It doesn't jump.

My mum gives me a glass of water. She tells me to put the bean at the back of my tongue. Then I have to drink the water all up and very fast. She says it's called a capsule. It helps to get rid of the evil inside.

"Don't chew it," she says.

She goes into the back room to give my brother his baby bottle. He gets medicine too. But he doesn't be evil. She puts it from a brown bottle into his milk. Then he drinks it all up. He doesn't eat food. It makes him sick from his tummy. My mum says his food got stuck and then it made him nearly die. So he got scared to eat it in case he died. My mum says he is little. My mum and dad shout about it sometimes.

My brother lies by the fire all day long. He is very tired. My dad says he shouldn't lie there. He gets mad about the fire.

"I don't have all the money to waste," he says.

Then my mum gets mad about it and she shouts at him and says all the bad words.

My brother has a coat. It is red. It's a baby coat. He keeps it all the time because he doesn't have a Mr. Ted. He hugs his coat all tight and drinks his milk. He takes it to playschool too. My dad says he is too soft. My mum says he should shut up. They fight about it. My dad says she is making him into a "soft lad."

I put the jumping bean in my mouth. I put it on my tongue. I drink all the water like my mum said. The jumping bean doesn't go away. I keep it in my mouth so my mum doesn't shout at me. I don't ask for more water.

She comes into the kitchen again and turns on the tap. She has to wash the plates. My mouth feels funny inside. It tastes all bad. I try to make it all go away. I try to make my mouth swallow it. But it doesn't want to. It makes me cough. I don't let the cough get out. My mum doesn't like it when I cough. I will give everyone germs.

The cough wants to come out very bad and I don't be able to stop it. I cough all loud and my mum turns around. The sick wants to come out again. I try but it doesn't be there. I start to cry and my head feels like it wants to pop into lots of bits and roll away. Maybe my eyes will pop out too. Like a big water balloon.

I cough very hard and my mum smacks my back but it doesn't go away. She gives me a glass of water.

"Drink it," she says.

I try to drink it all up but I keep coughing. The sick comes out and it goes all on the floor and on my clothes. I cry and tell my mum I am sorry. I didn't mean to get the sick on the floor. I try and make it get in the bin. I don't want the bad man to come because I was bad and made a mess.

All the sick gets out. I sit on the floor and tell my mum I am very sorry. It was on accident. I hug my knees all up and put my hands on my head. My mum is going to smack me for being all bad. She tells me to go into the backroom. I don't want to get up. She will hit me.

She doesn't hit me. She goes upstairs and I go to the backroom and stand still. I stand by the door. I wish I could get invisible and go away, but I'm not magic. She brings me new clothes and tells me to get dressed and go to school. I can't keep the crying away. I hug myself all tight and then my mum can hit me and make it all go away, like I do when I try to dig it all up with my Lego.

She tells me to go. My crying makes me have hiccups. It feels sad in my tummy. My mum is very mad at me. I walk to school and dig my fingers in my arms. I make it hurt bad.

"Stupid bad boy." I make it hurt and go away.

# TELLING TEDDY

## FOUR

*I got a bike Mr. Ted. It's all big and shiny and it was for my birthday. My mum remembered. But I got bad again. She didn't let me keep it. I'm sorry.*

I like Halloween time. It's spooky with lots and lots of monsters. Mr. Ted likes it too. We write lots of stories about it and draw pictures.

My friends all get to dress up. They knock on people's doors and get treats. They have to say trick or treat and then the people give them things. Or they get a trick played on them. Mr. Ted told me all about it. My dad says he isn't wasting the money to get a costume. He said I can go as I am because I look scary anyway with my stupid hair and dirty clothes. I don't be invited though.

Halloween is four days after my birthday. I count them. One, two, three, then Halloween. I don't count four. My mum and dad don't know it was my birthday. They forgot again.

It will be Bonfire Night soon too. My brother will get fireworks. If I am good then I get to watch them too. They make lots of banging noises and lots of colours in the sky. My teacher said my bonfire night picture was very good. I did it in lots of chalk on black paper. She sticked it on the wall.

My Nan likes the Catherine wheels. Me and Mr. Ted drew her one. My dad always throws them away because they aren't very good. They make the gate get burned and they fall on the ground.

It's the day after Halloween. I wake up and my mum and dad are not in the bed. They got up already and I didn't hear them. I didn't hear my dad's big bike.

I don't know if I am allowed to go downstairs. But my mum gets mad if I stay in bed too long. Me and Mr. Ted go downstairs. We can hear talking. I don't know who it is.

I go in the backroom. The bad man is sat at the big table. He has a big cup of tea. He says hello to me and he says my name. I say hello back and stand next to my brother. It feels funny in my tummy. My eyes want to cry. I didn't be bad.

The bad man smells funny as I walk past him. His coat smells like my dad's. I stay next to my brother. He is lied on the floor with his bottle and coat. He is watching television. I don't be allowed to watch it. I don't look, but I try not to look at the bad man.

He smiles at me. I don't like it. I don't like when he smiles at dark time. It's all scary. He smokes cigarettes. His cigarette looks funny. My mum and dad have white ones. His is brown.

My mum comes out of the kitchen. "Look at this," she says.

There is a bike behind the rocking chair. She pulls it out.

"This is for you," she says. "It's for your birthday."

I ask my mum really? She nods her head. I never had a bike before, not ever. The bike is silver. It has white wheels and white pedals. It has little wheels at the back. Maybe I can go and get a ride on it. The bad man stands up and takes the bike off my mum.

"These are stabilizers because you can't ride a bike yet."

I never got to ride a bike before. I never got anything for my birthday before too. I say thank you.

The bad man tells me to come and sit on it. He pushes the bike in front of him. I look at my mum about it. She nods her head.

The bike is too big. My feet can't get on the floor. I try to get off, but the bad man catches me. He tells me to stay. The bike is all wobbly because my legs are too small. The bad man tells me to put my toes on the floor. He has his arm around me. I don't like it. His beard is all scratchy on my neck. He puts his hand under the seat and makes it go down until my feet are on the floor.

My mum says I can ride my bike after school if I take my medicine. The bad man lets me go. I go into the kitchen with my mum. She gives me my jumping bean thing. I don't want to take the bean. I don't put it in my mouth. My mum folds her arms up. She has her mad face.

My mum takes the bean off me. She tells me to open my mouth and I shake my head.

"Do you want to be bad forever?" She asks.

## TELLING TEDDY

I make my head shake all about. I don't want to be bad. I listen for the bad man too. Maybe he will come in the kitchen. I stand near the back door. It is open. If he comes I am going to run away.

My mum grabs my head. She has her scratchy nails and puts them in my hair. It hurts. They are sharp. She has claws. She tries to push the bean in my mouth. But I don't open it.

She pushes it very hard. It makes my lip hurt and it gets inside. But I don't open my teeth. She lets the bean go and then I spit it in my hand. She hits me on the face. It stings and makes my teeth bash together. It makes me cry.

"Open your mouth," she says.

I shake my head, no. Maybe she will chop my mouth open. She puts her face close to mine and shouts at me very loud. She gets her spit on my face. I keep shaking my head. The bad man comes in the kitchen.

I tell Mr. Ted in my brain that I am sorry. I don't mean to be bad all the time.

My mum tells me to take it or else. I say no.

She digs her hand in my neck and shouts lots of bad words. Me and Mr. Ted talk in my brain. It's a secret. I close my eyes all up and count. One, two, three. We say four very fast. Five. We count all the way to nine. It's magic. To make me invisible. We count to nine three times. My mum smacks my legs and shakes me all up. But I don't get to feel it.

She drags me out the back door into the alley. She pushes me very hard and tells me to get away from her.

I go to school.

# J D STOCKHOLM

## FIVE

*I got to read to the little class today. It was so nice. I did it real good and the teacher gave me some chocolate. Maybe I be good now. Maybe the medicine works Mr. Ted.*

I like school. I get to be good and my teacher is nice. I don't have any friends there. Phillip and Anne go to a different school. But it's nice at my school too. My teacher gives me lots of stars. She tells me I am good.

My mum says the teacher gives me stars so I don't feel sad because she thinks I am stupid. My dad says she gives them to me because she likes little boys. But she likes the little girls too. She doesn't like me the bestest because I am a boy. I tell my dad that. He does the wink thing when he says it. Then he sticks his finger in his mouth. I don't look when he does that. He does it because I am bad.

I like getting lots of stars. I have lots and lots of them in my books. If I get to finish my work fast, my teacher gives me a star. Then she lets me read my reading book. I like to read lots of books. I get stars too when I finish one. My teacher says I read very good. My mum showed me how to do it. Then I could go away and not get on her nerves anymore.

I can count and say the alphabet too. I like the alphabet song. We sing it lots of times in the classroom. Sometimes it gets wrong and then the teacher has to stop. I don't get it wrong.

My Nan got me some books. They are a special kind. They get cassette tapes with them. I get a new one each two weeks. Then I listen to the story. Me and Mr. Ted read them together. We like the story about the witch and the cat and the mountain.

There is a story inside called Lord of the Flies. Me and Mr. Ted didn't read it yet. But we drawed pictures about it. Maybe the lord of the flies is a special fly with a cape and a crown. He gets to make the buzz noise in a posh voice. My Nan says I am silly.

At school I get to read with my class. I help the girl next to me. She doesn't know all the words. I show her about it. Then she covers some of the word and makes all the sounds. Then she can read it like I can.

My brother can't read. I show him too. My mum tells me off. She says that I am being a bully. But I don't be. I want to show him how to read. She gets my arm and drags me away. She tells me to sit on the chair and don't dare move. Then she tells my dad about it. He gets mad. I don't do anything right. Not ever. I tell Mr. Ted I am sorry. He tells me to be good. I try.

My teacher tells me to come to her desk. She says that I am good at reading. She asks if I like it a lot. I tell her yes and make my head nearly nod off. She asks if I want to read some books to the little class at lunch time. They don't get to play outside. They like stories too. I have a big smile on my face. I tell her yes please.

It's a rainy day today. We aren't allowed to play outside. I am glad. I don't get a coat because I am too big. I grow lots too fast. I am allowed to go and see the teacher and read to the little class.

The teacher smiles at me. She is very happy. She gives me a book. It is about Timmy, he goes to the dentist. I have read it already. She asks me if I can read it to the class. I say yes.

The children sit on the carpet. I sit on the big squishy chair like a teacher. I read the words. My voice feels funny. It makes me want to cough. I can see the teacher.

When me and Mr. Ted read at home. We make funny voices in our brains and funny faces. I do it as I read the book to the class. Then they get to laugh. I read like pretend.

I finish reading. The teacher tells me thank you. She asks me if I want to come back. I do.

"Wednesdays and Fridays?" She asks me. "Do you have a packed lunch?"

I shake my head.

"You can bring your school dinner here," she says. "They don't go into the big hall."

She gives me a little chocolate bar. I don't eat it. I think about the dinner. If I go to the classroom and read the books. I don't get seconds at dinner time. But maybe I get chocolate lots of times.

I say thank you and go back to my classroom. I put the chocolate in my bag. I want to take it home and show Mr. Ted.

# J D STOCKHOLM

I get home from school and sit by the chair in the backroom. I tell Mr. Ted about reading to the baby class. I don't tell my mum and dad. I don't be allowed to be with little kids. My mum says I give them my evilness. Then bad things get them. I don't want bad things to get them.

My brother has friends at playschool. My mum gets to sit in the kitchen with their mums. They come to our house for coffee. They talk about lots of boring things. I sit in the corner. I don't be allowed to play with my brother and his friends. If I get too bad, my mum tells me to go to the bedroom. I have to stay there until they are all gone. She doesn't want me to make them do bad things. Then she would have no friends. Everyone would say she has an evil son. I don't want my mum to be sad.

I don't tell my mum about the chocolate. I put it in a tin. My Nan gave me a tin. She keeped biscuits in it. Now I keep all my secret things in it. I hide my chocolate then my mum doesn't see. She says I am a thief. But I don't be. It's bad to steal. People that steal get sent to jail. My dad told me about it. They do bad things in jail. I only tell Mr. Ted about the chocolate.

I tell him not to be sad about reading. He didn't get to be there. But I will share my chocolate with him. Then he can be happy in his tummy too. We have to wait until my mum has gone out. She is going to the church. She gets ready and puts on a skirt. She wears lots of makeup. Her lips are all red. My dad gets to look after us.

She says night-night to my brother. She gives him a hug and a kiss.

"Behave," she says to me. I promise I will.

Me and Mr. Ted sit on the floor. I look at my chocolate. But we don't get to eat it yet. My mum goes out then my dad says it is bed time. He says he will read if I want. I tell him yes please. My dad reads books with lots of voices. I like when he reads.

I have to go to the toilet and then brush my teeth. My dad goes to the bedroom and gets my brother's pyjamas on him. He gets his baby bottle and his coat. I get Mr. Ted. He comes to the bathroom with me. He looks for the bad man so he doesn't come in the bathroom. We listen with all our ears.

We finish in the bathroom. I hug Mr. Ted and run all the way across the hallway. I keep my arms away from all the doors. Maybe the bad man is hiding. I don't want to look. Then he will get me and my dad won't hear it.

My dad gets in bed. My brother gets in next. Then me and then Mr. Ted. He lies at the edge. Then he can keep the bad man away.

My dad reads the book. I close my eyes. I listen to his words. It makes my eyes feel sleepy. My dad is reading about Noddy in Toy Town. He has a car and likes to help people. But then he gets lots of things wrong. Maybe he is like me. My eyes want to go to sleep. My brother makes lots of snore sounds. He lies with his bottle in his mouth, but it is all gone.

My dad gets up on the bed. He puts my brother on the pillows. He slides me down the bed. He takes my pants down and puts me on my tummy. I pretend to be asleep. He takes his clothes off too. Then he puts his thing inside.

It hurts. I don't be able to be quiet. My dad lies his head next to mine. He hugs me all tight.

"Breathe," he says.

Then he reads the book again.

My eyes cry. I don't be able to stop them. I try. I get them wiped on the bed. I talk to Mr. Ted in my brain. But the crying doesn't go away. My dad whispers the book words in my ear. He tries to make it not hurt very bad.

## SIX

*My mummy is right Mr. Ted. I am just bad inside. I pushed a girl over. Then I made her cry. I'm sorry. I don't want to be bad forever.*

My mum and dad don't get a lot of money to spend. My dad works lots. But my mum doesn't work anymore. She is too scared to be at work. So she stays home and looks after my brother. She says she has to look after my Nan. But my Nan is big and all grown up. She doesn't need to be looked after. She gets sad sometimes. She gets sad about my Gaga. She misses him a lot. I miss him too. I wish he didn't go to heaven.

It takes a long time for my mum and dad to get me some new clothes. They have to wait to get them from the other boy when he grows all big and then they don't fit him anymore. I grow too fast.

"You'll just have to do without like everyone else," my dad says.

My clothes are all too short. They don't go to my hands and feet. Sometimes I try to pull my jumper so that it makes my sleeves long. But my mum says that is bad and I will make them go out of shape.

My brother gets new clothes from a shop. He is little so his clothes don't cost lots of money. I wish I got to be little then I could get lots of new things too.

I got new shoes though. My Nan got them for me. They are blue and got monsters on the bottom. When I jump hard on the mud they make monster shapes. My Nan says it is funny. My Mum tells me that I don't be allowed to play in the mud or I will get too dirty. The monsters work on sand too. My mum didn't say I didn't get to play on sand.

It is winter time. So I don't be able to play on the beach. It is too cold and we have lots of gales and maybe I will get blowed away. We don't be allowed near the sea because the sea is too big and then it comes over the wall. My Nan says if I go passed the chains then I will get into trouble because the sea will wash me away.

I told my Nan that I can swim. But she said I don't be able to swim in the sea. I ask Mr. Ted about it. But he doesn't know. I don't know why I don't get to swim in the sea. I don't drown.

But it is too cold to be in the sea. My coat doesn't fasten. It is too little. The zip broke because I lifted my arms out and then it burst. My Mum said I have to suffer because I got it broken.

"It's your own fault."

I hug Mr. Ted. But he doesn't make me warm. He only has little fur. It keeps him warm. I wish I got fur.

At school my coat makes me cold. But we have to play outside for the dinner time and play time.

There is a wall inside the school. When we get bad we get to stand there and not be allowed to play with anyone. We have to stand there until lunch is all over and we go back to the classroom. The headmistress says that when we get naughty we don't deserve nice things like play time.

I don't like to be bad. But the evilness thinks about it. The wall has radiators on it. We get in a line to get lunch and we get to stand next to the wall and the radiators. I don't want to move. It is nice and warm. I keep my hands on them until it gets too hot and my skin is all red. It is my badness or the devil. He tells me to do bad things. My mum said the church is trying to fix it. That's why I take my medicine.

My mum's medicine makes me cold too. It makes me sleepy and cold. I wish I got to lie in bed and go to sleep. But I have to go to school.

My brother gets to stay home. He gets to lie by the fire all the time. My mum said the cold inside is my evil. She said it doesn't want to go away so it makes me feel bad inside.

I don't like to hurt other children. I don't like to make them cry. Sometimes I make my brother cry. It doesn't be on accident. But I get sad about it and make him better. Maybe I can make the children at school better if I get mean and make them cry. But I don't want to be told off. I don't want the teacher to telephone my mum and say I am bad.

I don't want to get in trouble and then the bad man gets me. But I am too cold. My nose is cold and so are my fingers and toes. I don't be able to stop shaking. Even my teeth bash together.

Lots of the other children have hats and scarves and gloves. There are some girls playing with a skipping rope. I don't know who they are. I just watch them because they play. One girl skips lots of times and the other children sing. I sneak over because they might know what I want to do and they will tell the teacher and I won't be sent to the wall. But they don't and I get close to the girl. I run and push her over. She falls on the floor and starts to cry.

She bashes her knee. I tell her I am sorry. I am bad inside. My evil is inside my tummy. I try not to let my eyes cry because of my badness. I tell the girl I am sorry lots of times. She gets up and goes to the dinner lady. She tells on me. Her friends tell on me too. They say I am bad and I pushed her over. The dinner lady asks me if I had done it. I don't say anything.

The dinner lady makes a tut noise. Like my Nan does when she isn't happy and then she shakes her head. She tells me to go and stand at the wall.

I stand with my hands behind my back. I lean on the radiator. It's nice and warm. I wish I don't have to go back to the classroom. I wish I could sleep at the radiator. All the children are outside. I watch them play. The girl is skipping again.

I am scared about going to my classroom. Maybe the dinner lady told my teacher and then she will shout at me about it. But she doesn't say anything.

I go home. I walk in the kitchen. My mum is there. She is making dinner. She doesn't shout at me. Maybe the dinner lady didn't call my mum.

I go into the backroom and sit next to my brother. Mr. Ted sits on my knee. I ask him about the girl. Maybe it is a secret and the dinner lady didn't tell anyone. Maybe the bad man doesn't know about it too.

Me and Mr. Ted play with my car and Larry the lamb. My mum brings the dinner in. It smells all nice. My dad's plate got another plate on top. He is still at work. My brother shakes his head. He doesn't want the dinner. My mum gives him a bottle. I wait for my dinner. But my mum sits down and eats her. She forgot again. Sometimes she forgets about it. I don't ask her because she gets mad. They don't have lots of money for food too.

## TELLING TEDDY

I open my tin and look at my special things. Me and Mr. Ted snap the chocolate. I give my brother some. He puts it in his mouth and watches his cartoons again. I put some in my mouth too. Then I be a statue so my mum doesn't see me eat it.

# J D STOCKHOLM

## SEVEN

*Mr. Ted. I got so bad. Now I don't be allowed to read to the little class. I'm very sorry Mr. Ted. I wish I could take it all away. I wish I didn't be bad anymore.*

I don't be bad on purpose. My evilness makes me do it. I don't mean to hurt the other children. I don't know how to make it all stop. I can feel my evil in my tummy. It feels all bad inside. My mum says it's because it's stuck inside and that is why I take medicine. To make it get out. But I don't know how to make it go away. I don't like the medicine. I don't like when the sick comes out my tummy all the time. It makes my throat all sore.

Lots of times I have been mean to the other children. It isn't their fault. It is mine. I am too bad and evil. I am good on the reading days. My evil goes away. But on Monday, Tuesday and Thursday I am all bad. I get the mean feeling in my tummy. Then my brain tells me to make one of the other kids cry. Then I get sent to the wall. I try to stop it. But I don't be able to.

I do it fast. Then I don't get to play outside. I eat my lunch. Then I eat seconds and then we all go outside and I be mean. I don't have to play outside in the cold.

There is a girl in my class. She is mean too. She is mean to me lots of times. She calls me stinky and stupid. She is stinky and stupid. She's got big stupid orange hair and big fat teeth. She is more stupider than I am. She has tickets for the trip. I don't be able to go because we don't have the money. But she is going. She shows me, then she laughs and says, "ha ha." She shouts ha ha very loud. Maybe I can bite her and say ha ha too.

I take the ticket out of her hand and then I rip it into a million pieces. I don't say ha ha. But I throw it on the ground and she cries.

"I can't go on the trip now," she says.

She runs off and tells the teacher. I get put on the wall again. I like being there and I don't be sorry. She isn't my friend anyway.

It is school finish time. We put our chairs on the table and then my teacher asks me to stay behind. I tell her I can't. I have to meet my mum at the shop. She will be mad if I am a long, long time. I am not allowed to do the dawdle thing.

## TELLING TEDDY

My teacher says it is okay. My mum already knows that I won't be going to the shop. My teacher tells me to follow her.

We got to the headmistress room. It has a big door at the top of the stairs. No one is allowed up there. Not ever. Only if the teacher says so.

My mum is sat in the headmistress's room. She is sat in a big chair. She looks at me. She has her mad face. I don't want to go in the room. My tummy tickles inside and I want to go to the toilet. But the teacher tells me I have to go in.

"Why are you hurting the other children at lunch time?" The headmistress asks me.

I don't know. I shrug my shoulders.

"Is someone being mean to you and that's why you do it?"

I shake my head.

"It isn't very nice to hurt other people," she says. "Your mum told me it makes her sad because you don't like to behave at home too. Your mum is very tired looking after your brother. You have to be a big boy and be good for your mum."

"My mum is the best mum ever. I don't like making her sad."

The headmistress nods her head too.

I don't know why I be bad. I tell Mr. Ted in my brain about it. Maybe it is because I don't let my mum give me the jumping bean thing. I close my eyes and promise to be good.

"I'll give you one more chance," the headmistress says. "But if you do it again, there will be consequences."

I don't know what consequences is. I will ask Mr. Ted when I get home. Or my dad. My dad knows all the words in the whole wide world. He learns them in books. He will tell me if I ask.

My mum and the headmistress talk about lots of things. I don't want to listen. It's boring things. I think about Mr. Ted. Maybe we can play when I get home.

My mum stands up and says thank you to the headmistress. I say thank you too. I promise to be good.

Me and my mum walk home.

"Do not walk with me," she says. "I'm sick and tired of all your behaviour."

She walks away very fast. I stand still. She isn't my friend anymore.

I walk home too. But I don't walk near her. I don't want her to be mad at me.

I don't get dinner too. My tummy isn't hungry anyway. I got lots of lunch at school.

My mum doesn't talk to me all night long.

My dad doesn't shout at me. We go to bed and my dad reads to me and my brother and Mr. Ted. My dad puts my brother on the pillow again. He takes my pants off and puts his thing inside again. But he doesn't make it hurt. Maybe Mr. Ted told him I was sorry about being bad.

# TELLING TEDDY

## EIGHT

*Mr. Ted. I turn everything to badness.*

I like the snow. It is crunchy under my monster boots. I jump and make shapes.

I am cold. I don't have my coat. All the other children got big coats on. I have my monster boots and shorts. I don't get pants because my mum and dad don't have lots of money.

I wish it was Wednesday. Then I get to read to the little class. Then I can be inside and be all warm.

My badness is inside. It's a scary monster in my tummy. I didn't get the sick all out this morning. My mum was asleep. She is very tired because she has lots of things to do.

I jump in the snow. But the snow is slidey. It makes me fall over. My shorts are all wet from the snow. It makes me lots of cold.

The big boy playing football laughs at me. Then he goes and plays with his friends again. My badness makes me do it. I go to the boy. Then I push him and call him a name and he falls over. Now he is wet in the snow too.

He gets up and says bad words to me. He runs to the dinner lady and tells her what I did. She tells me to go and stand at the wall. I don't care. I don't ever care. Now I get to be warm and he gets to be stupid.

The headmistress comes.

"Did you push the boy over?" she asks me.

I tell her yes.

"Why?"

I shrug my shoulders.

The headmistress is mad at me. She does the sigh thing like my dad. I look at my monster boots. Maybe they get to run very fast in the snow. Maybe I can run away.

She stands up and folds her arms.

"I don't think I have any other choice," she says. "If you can't be nice to the other children, then I have to not let you read to the class anymore."

I bite my teeth together. I don't let my eyes cry about it. I am a stupid boy. She will get mad if I cry.

She says I have to go and tell the teacher that I don't get to read for her class anymore. I don't want to. But the headmistress tells me I have to.

It feels scratchy inside. The headmistress tells me I have to go now. I have to follow her. We walk through the hall in the big side all the way to the little side. There is lots of lines on the floor. The floor makes a pattern. It goes sideways. I stand on them with my monster shoes. I count them. One, two, three…

The headmistress tells me something but I don't hear her. I count all the way to the little classroom. I can count to big numbers. I don't lose count.

The teacher is sat at her desk. I knock on the door and she tells me to come in. The headmistress stands outside. I don't say anything.

I bite my teeth very hard. But they don't stop it. My stupid eyes get out all the stupid tears and then it makes me cry. I don't be able to say the words. My tummy hurts inside. It is my badness. I wish it went away. Then I wouldn't be bad anymore. Then I wouldn't do all the bad things.

She gives me a tissue. Then I say the words. I tell her I am bad and I don't be allowed to read anymore. She has a sad face. She tells me that maybe if I can be good I will be allowed to come back and read. She has a smile.

I nod my head lots of times, but it doesn't fall off. I tell her I'll be good.

"I promise."

The headmistress takes me to my classroom. I sit in my wet shorts. The cold makes me shake all day long.

I walk home. I don't meet my mum today. She has to take my brother out with her friends. He gets to play. I look at the house when I walk up the alley. I can see my Gaga's old bedroom. Maybe the bad man hides in there. I have been bad. He knows about it.

I wait for my mum to come home. I stand by the back door. I don't be allowed to use the front door. But I hear her get home. The front door has chimes on it. They get banged when the door opens. I hear them. I stand up. My mum is in the backroom. My brother sits down to watch the television. He has got food from the chip shop. He likes those. They don't make him scared about eating.

## TELLING TEDDY

My mum opens the back door and lets me inside. She doesn't shout at me. The headmistress didn't tell her.

She tells me to go into the backroom and be quiet because my brother is eating. She didn't get me any chips. I don't want any. I am too bad to eat nice things. I don't hug Mr. Ted. I am too bad to get Mr. Ted hugs. He doesn't say anything about it.

I sit in the corner. I can smell my brother's chips. They have vinegar on them. They smell very nice. I get my Lego and put it on my tummy. I dig it all in to make it hurt. My tummy gets a red line and then it bleeds.

I am just a bad stupid boy that gets to be evil all the time.

I won't ever be good.

My dad comes home too. I hear his big giant motorbike. Then I see the back gate open through the window and he puts his bike in the shed. My mum goes outside to the shed. She has a cigarette in her mouth. She is shouting at my dad. She shouts at him about my badness at school.

My dad comes in the house. He comes in the back room.

"Stand up," he shouts at me.

I stand up and he does the stare thing.

"Well?" he says.

But I don't know what I have to say.

"Do you have something to tell me about school?"

My tummy has the sick inside. Maybe my badness wants to come out. I don't want to tell my dad about it. He will get all mad and then he will shout at me.

"Take your shorts off," my dad says.

I don't want to. I don't want him to do the hurt thing.

"I'm sorry," I tell my dad.

I can't stop the crying from coming out. I don't be able to help it. I tell him I won't ever do it again.

He keeps saying to take my shorts off. He says it loud and then he shouts in my face.

My hands shake lots. My head wants to pop because I cry very bad. I wish my dad knew I was very sorry. I tell him lots of times. I can't get my shorts off.

J D STOCKHOLM

My dad grabs my arm. He pulls my shorts down and pushes me at the wall. My shorts get stuck at my monster boots. I nearly fall on the floor.

I hear my dad's belt get open. I cry and tell him I am sorry. I don't want him to put his thing inside. He hits my bottom and my legs with his belt. It hurts very bad and I scream very loud. My brother starts to cry too. But my dad doesn't hit him.

My dad shouts at me and tells me to stop the crying. He hits me again with his belt. He shouts lots of times for me to 'shut the hell up.'

I bite my hand. Then I keep my cries inside.

My dad puts his belt back on then he goes outside to smoke a cigarette. I hug the wall. I am sorry for being bad.

## TELLING TEDDY

### NINE

*Mr. Ted. We were going to the church today to make me all better, but then I made it all bad again with my badness.*

My mum is sick of me. She likes to tell people the truth all the time. Because lies are bad to say. She thinks I am bad.

She doesn't let me play with Phillip and Anne because we are going to go to the church. My dad hasn't come home. He is out on his bike with his friends. My mum is mad because she got to find somewhere to take my brother. He has to go to my Nan's. He is too tired to come with us. My mum says he could lie on the floor at my Nan's house.

My mum gives him his medicine. It isn't like mine. It doesn't be made in the cow cup. He gets it like the capsule thing. They look like little balls. He has three of them. He doesn't be bad like me. He swallows his all up. But they don't make him get sick in his tummy. He doesn't have the evil inside like me. He is good. My mum says he has been alive before. But he had died in a fire and now that's why she got to look after him.

Maybe it hurt when he died in the fire. He doesn't remember. Maybe he is a ghost and he is magic and then he came back to life.

He doesn't need to go to the church to get better. So he is going to my Nan's and I have to go with my mum. The bad man is going to take us to the church. We are going in his big white car. It is a shiny car. She told the bad man thank you. She doesn't know what she was going to do with me anymore. She doesn't know what to do about my badness all the time. She doesn't like that she got called from the school teacher. That's why we have to go to the church, to try and make it better before it is too late and then I will just be bad forever.

My mum says it makes her sad. She doesn't want to have to send me away. But she doesn't know how she can keep me if I don't be good all the time. I don't want her to send me away. She has told me about the places that kids got to go. They live in a house with lots of kids. They are all bad and no one likes them. They don't have mums and dads to look after them and they don't get any friends. They don't even have toys. She said I won't be able to take Mr. Ted because he will get pulled to bits and put in the bin. I don't want Mr. Ted to be put in the bin. She said they got to use the kids as slaves. So we got to go to church to make it better.

I wait in the front garden. The bad man is smoking a cigarette. We wait for my mum. But I need to go to the toilet. I don't be allowed to go to the one in the back garden. My mum has made the back door all locked up and she will be mad if I make her open it again. The bad man says maybe I should use the one in the house. I didn't tell him I need the toilet. Maybe he read it in my brain.

I go into the hallway. My mum is upstairs. I can hear her. The bad man is outside. He isn't upstairs. But I don't want to go in case he comes too. Then I don't be able to get away.

But I really need to go to the toilet. I stand in the corner. It is next to the door that is the front room. I don't be allowed to go in there. It has my Gaga's things inside. From when my Nan and my Gaga lived in this house. It is their house. But my Nan lets my mum live in it because she got sick that time when my big brother was thrown at the fire. My Nan lives in a special place. So she gets looked after. She says she will come back and live with us soon.

I am bursting to go. I let it out slow in the corner. Then no one can see it.

I don't be able to see it on the floor. And I don't see on my pants. But my mum comes down the stairs and she sees it. She asks me why I didn't go and use the toilet. The bad man comes in too. He tells my mum I went in the house to use the toilet. She asks me why I didn't because it is just at the top of the stairs. I don't know why. I shrug my shoulders. My mum says lots of bad words.

The bad man goes to lock his car. We don't be able to go to the church. My mum has to make me clean and change my clothes. So we are too late to go to the church. My mum tells me to go upstairs to the bathroom. She puts the cold water in the bath and takes my clothes off.

"Stand in the bath," she says.

She isn't very happy that she has to make me all clean again. She isn't happy that she got to miss the church too.

"Brother Marcus isn't going to be happy about us missing today," she says.

## TELLING TEDDY

The bad man comes upstairs. I don't like that he stands at the door and talks to my mum. I get scared in my tummy because he is there. My mum tells me to get out of the bath and then she says she has to go to call the church. I don't want her to go downstairs but she does.

I don't have my clothes on. The bad man is by the door. He has his big smile. He comes in the bathroom and grabs my arm. I shout for my mum.

The bad man pushes me against the wall. He pushes my arm all the way up my back. It nearly touches my head. Maybe he is going to make it come off. It feels like it is going to come off my shoulder. Like when I get bad and pull the arm off my brother's toy soldiers.

The bad man has to hurt me because I am too bad. He bites my shoulder and then he scratches all on my legs and my tummy. He bites me lots of times. He puts his thing inside and makes it hurt very bad. I shout my mum, but she doesn't hear me. There is blood down my legs. The bad man tells me I have to get in the cold water to get clean.

## TEN

*Mr. Ted. I'm sorry. I didn't mean to be bad and make my dad hurt my mum; please tell her I'm sorry.*

My mum brings me some clothes. I get dressed and she says I have to go downstairs and sit on the chair at the dinner table. We don't be eating. I just have to sit there because I am too bad and she tells me I don't get to move.

It hurts to sit on the chair. The bad man had scratched and bited me. They hurt too. Like little ants on my skin with sharp teeth. Sometimes I draw them in my book. Mr. Ted gets them squashed.

I don't look at the bad man or my mum. I just look at my hands. The bad man didn't pull my arm off. But it still hurts. I don't have Mr. Ted. He is upstairs in bed. I wish he was with me. Then I could get to hug him. I don't ever get to hug anyone. I don't be able to stop my eyes from crying. I don't let my mum see.

The bad man sits at the table. My mum has to wash my clothes. She puts them in a bucket. The bad man smokes a cigarette. I don't like the smoke. It smells all bad.

"Back to school on Monday?" He asks me.

I nod my head a little bit. Then the tears don't get to fall out and he won't get mad.

My mum says she has to telephone my dad because we don't go to the church. The bad man says he should go home. My mum says I have to tell him I am sorry for wasting his time.

I shake my head.

"Don't be so rude," she says.

I whisper, "I am sorry."

My dad is home. He is mad. He is mad because my mum had called him and he has to come home and deal with me. He shouts at my mum. My mum and dad shout in the garden at each other. I cover my ears.

My dad comes into the house. He hits me with the back of his hand on my face. I fall over and the table stops me getting on the floor.

"I'm sorry," I tell my dad.

## TELLING TEDDY

He shouts at me and asks me about going to the toilet. I tell him I don't know. He calls me lots of bad names. He says that I am never good and that they wish they got a different boy because I don't be good.

Ever.

My dad is mad because I don't know. He pulls me off the chair with my hair. I try to get his hand off. But he has his fingers in it and then he pulls me and makes me stand up.

"Don't you dare cry," he says.

I don't be able to help it. Maybe he is going to pull my hair off. It feels like he is going to make my head pull open.

He drags me into the hallway. I don't want to go upstairs. I don't want him to hurt me for being bad. The bad man hurt me already. I am all sore inside. My dad makes me walk and it hurts.

I don't get to stop crying. I cry all the way up the stairs. I ask my dad to please not put me upstairs in the bedroom. But he does and he hits me across the face and lets go of me. I fall to the floor.

"Stop being a baby," he says.

He tells me he hates me so bad and wishes that I don't be there.

"You ruined my life."

I know I am bad. I know I make his day sad. He hates me. He tells me he does. Maybe I can go away and they will be happy. I wish I could go away. I am sorry I am so bad.

My dad tells me I should go and play with the moving cars and trams and make everyone happy.

He says that I should listen.

"It's going to be all your fault. You made it happen."

I don't know what is my fault. He closes the door and goes downstairs.

I don't get off the floor. My dad left me there. I squash myself under the bed. My mum and dad shout very loud. I put my hands on my ears. But it doesn't work. I still get to hear all the bad words. I get to hear my dad hit my mum. Everything makes lots of crash noises and she screams.

I hear the door bang. And then I hear his big motorbike make its growl sound.

I stay there on the floor for a long, long time. It is nearly dark. My mum puts my brother to bed and gets a bath. I get my pyjamas on and get into bed. She doesn't know I am awake. I lie behind her when she gets in bed too. I tell her in my brain that I am sorry for being bad. I am sorry I made my dad hurt her.

It is all my fault.

# TELLING TEDDY

## ELEVEN

*Mr. Ted. I rided my bike today. I did it. My mum showed me. I got to ride it and I didn't touch the ground. Not once.*

I open my eyes. It's morning time. My dad doesn't be in the bed. I wake up when my mum gets out of the bed. She doesn't talk to me. I lie there and hug Mr. Ted. I don't tell my mum I am awake. Maybe she is mad at me because my dad hurt her and it was all my fault. My evilness always got the bad things to happen. I wish I knew how to make them all go away. I wish my mum didn't get to cry and be hurt all the time.

My mum gets out of bed. She goes to the bathroom. Me and Mr. Ted sit up. We listen for the bad man. But there doesn't be anyone else. I open my mum's cream. It is for her face. Mr. Ted smells it. It gets on his fur. We put the cream away and then we don't get in trouble.

My mum comes back again when she has got all her things done. Everyone has to brush their teeth when they get up. That's what my Nan says. We have to get out of bed. Go to the toilet and then get our teeth cleaned. She says that's what I've got to do every day. Then I have nice shiny teeth.

My mum sits on the bed. She puts the cream on her hands and her face. They smell like coconut and sunshine. Mr. Ted smells like coconut and sunshine too. He smells like my mum. I hug him tight. We pretend to be asleep.

Me and Mr. Ted are pretending because my mum gets mad at me that she doesn't be able to get the time to herself. I always wait until my mum says I am allowed to wake up. I don't know if my mum wants me to wake up. Sometimes my mum gets mad because I don't wake up first.

Maybe it is because I have the brains like a hen. My mum says I should know these things by now. But I don't.

My mum gets out of the bedroom and she's got to do lots of things. I hear her. She goes downstairs and then comes back up again. She is talking to someone on the telephone. Maybe it is my Nan because she is talking about my brother. He is still in the bed too. But he sleeps lots all the time. Not even the house exploding into millions of pieces can wake him up. That's what my Nan says. Even his wee doesn't wake him up. He needs to wear nappies at night because he always gets wee in the bed, but he is too big for them.

My mum wakes my brother up. She shouts at me to get up and get out of bed. I do it my fastest. I go to the bathroom and use the toilet. And then I brush my teeth. I get my clothes on and I wait for my mum to say I can go down the stairs.

My mum has a mark on her face. Sometimes, I get them when my dad gets mad at me and then he smacks me because I am bad. I get them lots of times on my arms and legs from the bad man. My mum says they are because I am clumsy. Like Humpty Dumpty.

Sometimes, I press them. It hurts when I do that. But I like to do it. I pick at all the cuts too. When I pick the ones on my knees, my Nan says if I do that then they don't get better. But they do. My Nan just doesn't know about it.

My mum doesn't talk to me. She lies my brother on the floor by the fire and puts the cartoons on for him. He is very lucky to watch the television all the time. I wish I got to watch it. I like it. He hugs his coat and then I have to go in the kitchen.

My mum gets my brother's medicine and she puts it on a little plate with four chocolate biscuits. That is all he likes to eat. He doesn't really like the other stuff. I don't get any because I can eat everything else my mum says. When I am all growed I can have chocolate biscuits for breakfast. But I don't get anything. I don't eat breakfast any more. My mum keeps forgetting to give it to me. I wish I had it sometimes. The sick is hard to come out because I don't have the food. Sometimes, there is not a lot of sick in my tummy.

I don't get to go to school today. My mum says we are going to the church later and she doesn't want me getting into any more trouble. I don't mean to get into trouble all the time. My mum says I have to be good at the church. I promise her that I will.

I have my medicine. Then I get a little bit of sick in the bin. I don't get it on the floor or my shoes. I ask my mum if I can go and play outside on my bike. I don't be able to ride it yet with the big wheels. But my dad has taken them off. He says that I should be able to ride the bike with just two wheels like he can.

But I don't dare let both my feet off the ground. I take my bike into the alley way at the back of the house. I try to make the bike move. I push the ground with both my feet. But it doesn't get very good. I am not good at bikes like my dad. I try to get my feet to go onto the pedals. But then the bike just falls over because it is too wobbly. I wish I can ride bikes like my dad. He can ride any bike in the world.

My mum comes outside. She stands by the gate and smokes her cigarette. She looks like her eyes have got crying inside them. They are all wet. But she isn't crying. She sits on the step at the back gate. I ask my mum if she is okay. She nods her head. I hug my mum. She doesn't hug me. She still smokes her cigarette.

"Your dad gets mad and then he loses his temper," she says. "It's his stupid friends. They make him this way."

She wishes he is nice like the doctor. Then maybe she can get to be happy.

"Maybe you can get married," I tell my mum.

"I will one day. Gaga said he was meant for me."

My evilness is in my tummy. It makes me say the bad things again. Lies are bad. They come from the Devil. But I don't be able to stop it.

"I have seen the doctor," I tell her. "He got passed our house. In his big car like Batman."

My mum gets a big giant smile on her face.

"When did you see him? Today?"

I nod my head all big. "When I got my bike outside."

"Are you sure?"

I nod lots of times. Like a big nod promise.

I close my eyes and make the picture of the car in my brain. I tell my mum what it looks like. She lights another cigarette.

"Maybe he came down here because he knows it's school time and he wanted to see me before he went to work," my mum says.

Her voice got all fast. She talks about the doctor. But she calls him Batman in case anyone is listening. It's a secret.

My mum is very happy. I get back on my bike.

"If you put one foot on the pedal then you will be able to ride the bike," she says.

I don't know what she means. I put one foot on a pedal, but I don't move.

"Push the pedal down and then lift your other foot."

I do what she says, the bike goes front ways. It wobbles and I put my foot back on the ground.

"Keep doing it," she says.

There is lots of bats in my tummy like my Nan calls them. They tickle because the bike gets to move and I don't put my feet on the ground. The bike goes all the way from the house to the big shed in the alley. I turn around to show my mum. She isn't there.

I look at the back gate. Maybe my mum just went to make sure my brother was okay. Sometimes, she does because he is just little. She likes to make sure he doesn't get into bad things. I get into bad things. That's all I ever do, she says, but not him. He is good and then she has to check on him all the time. Maybe she is scared my badness will get him. It won't, not ever. I won't let it. He doesn't be bad like me. The bad man doesn't hurt him. And my dad doesn't hurt him or smack him or tell him off. He is good inside.

I can feel my evilness. I wish I could make it go away. I ask Mr. Ted. But he doesn't know how to do it. Maybe when I get to be a doctor I can.

My brother would be sad and cry if he got my badness. When he gets told off he gets sad about it. My mum gives him a hug to make it all better. He doesn't be like me she said. I am harder than he is. She says I got to be new to the earth. God just made me and then the Devil gets to talk to me because I don't know how to keep him away. So I didn't understand like my brother does. Because my brother has been alive before. So he is more special and it makes him sad sometimes.

My mum doesn't come back outside. I wait forever. I kick the pedal on my bike and make it go backwards. But she still doesn't come. Maybe she forgot I am there. Maybe I just don't be good on the bike.

I go back to the house. I ride my bike and I don't touch the ground. Not once. I get all the way to the gate and I don't get my feet down. I can to ride my bike. I don't be allowed to ride it into the garden. So I get off it and put it back in the shed. It doesn't be allowed in the house either.

## TELLING TEDDY

My mum is in the house. She is drinking tea. She is sat at the dinner table. She is sat in the back room at the dinner table with the bad man.

# J D STOCKHOLM

## TWELVE

*We are going to a new church today Mr. Ted. My mum says you can come too. It's to fix my badness.*

The bad man sits at the dinner table. He doesn't be eating. He has my dad's cup and is drinking my dad's tea. He says that he saw me play on my bike.

"You got good at riding on it," he says.

I nod very fast. He says that I am a good boy. I didn't know that he had got to see me on the bike. The bad man just sneaks up on me in the bedroom.

Not outside.

The bad man doesn't ever say I am good. He only comes when I get bad.

We are going to church today. I am not allowed to wee in the hallway. Or do anything bad. The bad man is taking us. The bad man likes the church too. He asks me about the things I do at school. Inside my tummy it gets all hot and I feel it flop around. Maybe the sick is going to come out. Or it might be the bats inside. The bad man got to know about my badness at school. Maybe Mr. Ted can tell him that I got to be sorry about it.

Maybe the bad man knows about the bad things I said to make my mum happy. It is bad to tell fibs. I am a big fat fibber. The bad man can read minds. Maybe he knows what I got to say to her and then he is going to make it hurt. Maybe my dad will make it hurt. I don't like it if the bad man has been and then my dad did the hurt thing too. I don't be able to keep the crying away because then it gets to hurt even if my dad doesn't make it hurt.

The bad man asks me why I got bad at school. I shrug my shoulders and go to sit next to my brother. He is sleeping. He is too tired all the time. My Nan says he looks like a sleeping ghost.

When she comes to the house, she picks him up. But my mum gets mad about it. She tells my brother that my Nan is bad and he shouldn't let her. So my brother doesn't like my Nan. He tells her to go away lots. He uses bad words like my mum and dad. It makes my Nan sad. But I make my brother cry because I smack him for using bad words all the time.

# TELLING TEDDY

We are going to a new church far away. My mum says I can take Mr. Ted and the bad man gives me some comics like the ones that are in the doctor's place. But these got to be new. They still got the sweet and the toy stuck to the front. My mum says I can have it. But I don't be allowed to make a mess.

The bad man has to carry my brother and put him in the back of the car. I get scared. Maybe the bad man will hurt my brother if he gets mad. But the bad man doesn't. He just puts him in the car and gives him the coat and the baby bottle. We take my brother to my Nan's. I don't be allowed to get out of the car and see her. But she looks in the car and tells me to be a good boy. She kisses me and gets her pink lipstick on my face. It doesn't be on accident. She laughs and I try to get it off.

It is a long drive to the church place. It is boring in the car. I am too hot. But I don't ask my mum to get the window open. She always says no. I play games with Mr. Ted. I play them on pretend in my brain. Mr. Ted can still hear me. But not my Mum. She doesn't like it when I play games. She says I am being a baby. So I don't let her know that I like to. We play I-spy. But he doesn't be very good at it. He doesn't know the names of lots of things. Sometimes when we don't know names we make them up.

We read the comics too. But we fall to sleep. The car makes us do it. It makes my eyes want to close. I don't be able to stop them.

I open my eyes and it is dark time. I am in the car. But it isn't moving and my mum and the bad man are gone.

There is a house. It is big and I have never seen it before. The lights are all on and the door is open. There are people inside. But I don't see my mum or the bad man.

The house looks like a big castle. It has lots of stones on the walls outside. It also got an axe and some wood. Maybe they chop people's heads off. But I don't see any. I don't know if I am allowed to be out of the car. My mum didn't say. She has to tell me if I be allowed. Maybe she did when I was asleep and I just don't remember about it. There are lots of people like a party. I didn't ever go to a party before.

Maybe my mum doesn't want me to wake up. Like she doesn't sometimes with my brother. She leaves us lots of times in the car, and then he wakes up and makes me mad. Inside, my badness makes me nip his leg and make him cry. But then I hug him better because it is just the badness. It isn't me. I don't like it when he cries. It feels like forever when we got to wait.

Maybe my mum is leaving me in the car until I wake myself up. I get out of the car. And I walk to the house. My mum isn't there with the other people. They are all smoking cigarettes. A man tells me that my mum is through the kitchen. She is in a different room.

I go where the man said. My head feels tired inside. I want to lie back in the car and get to sleep. But I want to find my mum and go home because I am too tired. My mum is sat on the sofa. She is by a fire. It is real. Not like the one we have at home. The one at home in the backroom has a button and we have to use matches. It makes me scared when my mum lights it because maybe it will burn her fingers. But it doesn't ever do that. My Nan says I don't be allowed to touch it. I am never ever allowed to press the button because it has some gas. She said it is like dentist gas and will make everyone fall to sleep and then no one will wake us up; we will sleep forever.

Sometimes I press it. It makes a funny hiss and smells funny. It doesn't ever make me fall to sleep.

The fire next to my mum looks like they got a bonfire in the house. Like on bonfire night when all the fireworks got set off and there are big fires and they throw Guy Fawkes into the fire because he is too bad. He tried to set fire to the bosses of the world.

My mum said we are going to go for a walk.

"Everyone is going, like an adventure," she says.

I like adventures. I read about them in my books.

My mum says I have to get a torch. But I don't be allowed to mess about with it or they will make me not have it and I will have to see in the dark. I don't be able to see in the dark.

## TELLING TEDDY

### THIRTEEN

*Mr. Ted. We was at the new church place. We went in the forest, but I don't remember it. I have lots of bad pictures in my brain about it. I nearly made my mum go away forever.*

The house is in the countryside. It smells like farms and cow poo. But I don't see any farms or cows. There are just lots and lots of trees. It looks like something in one of the stories where the monsters and lions live. Maybe I can find a lion. But it is dark in there. We walk to the trees and I get my torch and make them all light up. It is spooky in there. We can do lots of scary jumping out like I do to my Nan. It is a forest. I have never seen so many trees before.

My mum walks behind me. My eyes can see lots. Maybe it is like Superman. He got to be able to see in the dark. But I don't have a cape. I don't like my cape. The bad man used it. I don't like thinking about the bad man. It makes me scared then my brain sees lots of pictures about the bad man and the bathroom.

I get my torch and I am faster than everyone else. They are all grownups and slow coaches. But I am fast and play on the logs and leaves and things. The leaves have all fallen off the trees. I like to run and kick them in big piles. We walk for a long time. I don't know where we are going. Or if we're nearly there yet. I just play. Mr. Ted is with me.

Me and Mr. Ted talk about lots of things. He wants to know where we are going. He says I should ask my mum. I turn around. But there is no one there. Not even my mum or the bad man or anyone else. They are all gone. It is just me and Mr. Ted. I didn't hear them go away.

I go back the way I walked from before. The way we got from the house. But it is just lots and lots of trees. I am sleepy too. In my head. My eyes don't want to be open. Maybe I fell asleep when I walk. It feels like it. Because then I got to wake up.

Maybe I sleep walked. Maybe I did it with my arms out like a monster. I don't know. I can't remember. The pictures in my brain are dark.

I shout my Mum. I don't want to shout very loud because I don't want to make lots of noise and get in trouble. But no one hears me. I shout some more. But there is still no one. I walk very far. It makes my head all in circles. It is all dizzy inside of it. I wish I was at the house then I can lie by the fire and go to sleep. I am cold inside.

My tummy hurts. I keep shouting my mum. I take in lots of breath and make it sound as loud as I can. I keep shouting and shouting. But no one comes. I cry. I don't be able to stop it. I try to scream for my mum. I am scared. But no one comes to help me.

My Nan said if I got lost, then I have to stay where I am and not move. But I don't like where I am. It got dark and there are lots of trees and no one will ever find me. I don't be able to stop shouting. I stand and shout lots of times. I just keep doing it. Inside my tummy and where my heart got to be, feels all cold in there. It squeezes up lots. Like the badness is making them jump around.

My brain gets all funny inside. I am sat. I don't know when I got to sit. Maybe I have been daydreaming. Maybe I had falled to sleep. There is a lady there. The one from the church. The one with the fish. I don't know how she got there. I didn't know where she came from. She got there when I was sleeping and I didn't hear her.

I don't remember lots of things. But there are lots of pictures in my brain. The picture is me and my Mum and the people at the house. They tell me to pick something. I have to pick the left or the right. But I don't know and I choose wrong. And then my mum got to be gone and I was never going to see her again. Because I sent her away. Maybe I made her go to heaven.

I don't know where I am. I hug Mr. Ted. I don't have my torch. It has got lost somewhere. But I don't remember. Maybe I have been to sleep for a long, long time. The pictures keep playing in my brain. I don't like when pictures do that. It makes me think about the place when there is blood. It got to be all the same people again. There are lots of pictures. I don't like them.

"I can't find my mum," I tell her.

"If you promise to be good, you can find her again," she says.

## TELLING TEDDY

I nod my head and crossed my heart and hoped to die. "I won't ever be bad again."

Maybe if I be bad, my mum will go away forever.

The lady tells me to follow her. I don't know where we walk to. I can't stop my crying and I keep shaking. I try to hug Mr. Ted to make it all go away. But it doesn't. My head hurts very bad inside.

My mum is at the house where we had been before. I run my fastest to where she is. She stands smoking a cigarette. I squeeze her with my hug. She doesn't be gone forever.

"Get off," she says.

But I don't want to. She gets my hands and makes me not hug her. Me and Mr. Ted sit on the floor. He sits on my legs. But I squeeze him up because I got my legs up. I put my head on my knees and then I put my hands in the front of my hair and pull it very, very hard until it makes my crying go away. I am too bad to cry. Too bad to have a mummy.

## FOURTEEN

*Mr. Ted. I promise to be good. Always.*

I am going to be a good boy. Like they said at the church; the people there. The lady with the fishes from the church house when I went with my mum. She told me I got to be good and I try my bestest all the time. I don't ever want my mum to go away. Not because I am too bad. I don't let the badness get in my brain. Then no one got to hurt me and I don't get taken away. I promise I am going to be good all the time for my mum and dad. I will never be bad again.

The bad pictures keep being in my brain all the time. I close my eyes. They don't want to go away. They make me cry at night times. But I don't tell my mum. She will be mad at me about it. She already told to me that I have lessons to learn. I am a new soul she says. I don't know what that means. But I don't like the pictures. They make me scared all the time. I don't know how to make them stop.

They make me want to hug Mr. Ted and cry. They are too scary to think about. I don't like them. Maybe my evilness makes lots of stupid nightmares in my head. They feel like lots of bad things all the time.

I am scared because I can feel the bugs on me like I did at the church place. But there are lots of them. I want to make them go away. The man at the church said I can't move because then they got to bite me. They bited bad boys. I didn't want them to do that. I didn't be able to get away because they got my hands all tied up and I didn't get any clothes on. The bugs made my skin feel funny and made me want to cry. I don't like thinking about them. But my brain keeps doing it. I wish it got to go away.

I don't know why my brain makes the bad pictures. I don't remember getting any bugs on me. I don't remember anything. Maybe it was like pretend with the pictures. Maybe my badness makes me see the bad things. I don't tell Mr. Ted because they got the bugs and things and made them hurt inside like the bad man did with his thing. It still hurts after. It makes it get too sore to walk. I keep thinking there are bugs in my pants. Maybe Mr. Ted will think I am stupid like everyone else does.

## TELLING TEDDY

Dreams don't be real.

Me and my dad are going to the library. He said I can come because I have been good. I keep myself quiet because I don't want to be bad. I try to look at all the books. Maybe I can make them make the bad pictures go away. My dad lets me pick lots of books. I was good for lots of days so I get lots of Mr. Men books too. They make a huge big pile.

I am good for my Nan too. She has to go to a place. It is a nice place that stops her being sad. She is sad because my Gaga is in heaven and she misses him lots of times. The place helps her to get friends so she doesn't miss him too much. She gets to paint and draw and make cakes and lots of fun things. She has lots of friends too. They are all nice when I get to go there too. They always talk to me. But I get shy.

They are doing a market thing and my Nan is going to be selling cakes. She asked if I wanted to help, and I do. She asked my mum. My mum said yes. I don't get any money for it. But I get to help out and it will make me a good boy if I do. I want to. Like I promised. I will be good. I have to be good all the time so the badness never comes again.

I get to go with her and help. I get to sit and help sell the cakes to the people that come in. It is called a flea market. I don't know why it was called a flea market. I ask Mr. Ted. He doesn't know. It is a funny name. I ask my dad but he says it is because they sell fleas. He says all old ladies have fleas and that I got them too.

I don't have fleas.

I think my dad is silly sometimes. He tells me that eggs growed on trees. I know they don't. But I don't be able to get my dad to believe me. I even show him a picture of a chicken. But he says I am wrong. I ask my dad if he is telling tales. But he says he doesn't. He draws me an egg tree. I tell him I don't ever see an egg tree and he says that is because the trolls taked them all the time. I think my dad is a fibber.

My dad asks me if my Nan makes the cakes. I tell him that they all got to make them. My Nan had told me they get a day and they all make lots and lots of cakes together to sell for the market. My dad asks me how do old ladies got the eggs from the tree? He says they got to be too old to be climbing trees. I tell him that they didn't and he asks how they make their cakes. He makes me get mad in my tummy. He doesn't listen about the chicken.

I get my arms folded and give him my mean face. Like when the teacher at school wanted everyone to get quiet. But my dad says to stop it and that maybe I have that face because my fleas make me get itchy.

I don't have fleas.

I tell my dad that the old ladies use eggs from chickens. He says chickens don't lay eggs. He says maybe chicken cakes would taste funny.

I stop talking to him.

## TELLING TEDDY

## FIFTEEN

*Mr. Ted. I make sure I do everything just right. Just like I promise. I am a good boy.*

I help my Nan. We have to sell lots of cakes. Lots of people come in and buy lots of things. My Nan doesn't let me do the money part. I want to. Like a shopkeeper, but she says I can't. I get to put the cakes in the bag and give it to the people.

My Nan gives me some pennies that I get to spend. She lets me go and look at the other places. They are called stalls. I look at the book stall.

"Buy anything you want," she says.

I buy some books and some cars that are there. My Nan says I can take them home if I am a good boy. I am good. I promise. I will always be good now. I make sure I am. I don't let my badness get out.

I always make sure I get all the things right. Then I don't ever be bad again. In the mornings, I always get to brush my teeth. I count when I do it. Then I don't take lots of time. My mum gets mad if I am too long so I don't want to make her shout at me. I count to sixty and then I am finished. Then I put my brush back. I put it the right way around like before I taked it out. Then I get the mess out of the sink so it looks all clean and shiny. If it doesn't be cleaning day my mum gets mad about it and then she has to clean everything with the cleaning powder. She shouts about all the hard work she has to do and my badness makes her get more work. I don't get my badness out ever again.

I have to make a sound because I count a lot. My dad says if I keep doing things like that people will think I am crazy. He keeps telling me to stop it. But I don't want to make anything bad happen and then send my mum away.

"Only crazy people count and click all the time," he says.

I am not crazy. I just have to be good.

When I get my clothes on in the morning; my pyjamas all get folded up nice and neat like my mum wants me to. My slippers have to be the right way around and then they don't be uneven. We learned about that at school. When things are all the same it is even.

## J D STOCKHOLM

When my mum gives me the medicine; I stand in the same place every day. Unless she tells me I have to go somewhere else. But I don't. I make my feet be together the same. I remember it all the time. I don't move at all and I swallow the medicine all up. Then I count until I get to one hundred and make myself get the sick out of my tummy if it doesn't want to come out itself. I get it right in the bin all the time. It is good to do that. Then my mum doesn't get to clean up and I don't get to be bad.

I walk to school. I don't meet Phillip and Anne. I just go to school. I count all the steps there so I don't be slow and get late and then get told off.

I am good at dark time too. Sometimes if my bad thoughts get in my brain. Then I get something and make it hurt. I do it right away. I do it six times because six is a good number. If I get over six I start again. Sometimes my brain gets tired or the bad thoughts or nasty pictures get there and then I don't know how many. I have to start all again. I don't know that it makes my arms and legs bleed lots. But I don't get it on my clothes.

Mr. Ted tells the bad man he doesn't need to come. He tells him that I already get the hurt part. The bad man doesn't come every night. Just sometimes. When my dad is out. Maybe the bad man is scared of my dad.

I am a good boy for my dad too. He always says I am. He whispers in my ear when he reads the books to me. He says that I am a good boy. I don't let my eyes cry. I lie there and bite my mouth. I pretend to be asleep. My dad reads books and my brother has to sleep on the pillows. But my dad doesn't know my eyes cry. It is bad if I do. Maybe then he will get mad at me for it.

My dad made a new game too. I don't ever be bad about it but I don't like it. I pretend I am in a story. My dad doesn't know I am there too. He puts his thing in my mouth. But not like the bad man. He doesn't sit on me and make me squashed. He doesn't be mean to me and make my head bash on the wall. I don't be bad. My evil doesn't come out.

His thing does the same as the bad man's. It gets the yucky stuff in my mouth. I don't like it very much. It tastes bad. It makes my throat want to be sick. My dad gets my face and smiles at me. He says not to let the sick out. I don't. I make it all stay down in my tummy. I am a good boy.

# TELLING TEDDY

# J D STOCKHOLM

## SIXTEEN

*Mr. Ted. I sat on the box all night long. I didn't make any noise.*
*I was very good.*

Sometimes, my Nan says that my brother is a lazy bones. She laughs and jokes when he lies on the floor all the time. She asks him why he didn't play, but he says he is too tired and wants to watch the television. She says he will make his eyes all square. He will get to look funny with square eyes.

Because he is a lazy bones. He doesn't get up at the morning time. He stays in bed and sleeps a long, long time. My dad says it is because he is awake lots at the night time. He doesn't be a big boy and he wees in his bed every night. He does it sometimes lots. They don't get nappies for him because only babies get nappies. But he does have a baby bottle with the milk in it. Maybe he thinks he is still a baby.

My mum is very tired. When my brother gets his wee in the bed at night time. She has to get up and make the bed all nice and dry again. It makes her get very tired. Once I asked if she got to be a lazy bones too, but my dad smacked me for saying it. He says I am lazy. I didn't know it is bad words to say. I told them that I am sorry. And I told Mr. Ted too.

My mum isn't lazy because she has to do lots of things for me and my brother all the time. She has to make the house all nice and tidy too. She says it takes a long time every day and then she is tired and goes to bed. But when she wakes up it has to start all over again. Maybe it is lots of boring things to do.

My dad has a new job too. He doesn't have to get up very early. He works in a new garage. It has a big ramp like the one I have for my cars. His is big and giant and it lifts up the real cars. I like to stand under the real cars. They look all exciting under them. But he has to lift them up so he doesn't have to lie on the floor. He likes his new garage. And he doesn't have to go to work until I have to be at school. So he can sleep in the bed longer.

I get up. Everyone is still fast asleep. But I have to go to school and do all my things all by myself. I wore pyjamas at bed time and didn't sleep in my day time clothes. I sat at the box by the window and didn't make any sound. My dad says I make too much noise with all my faffing about.

I have to sit all quiet. I listen for a long time for the bad man's shoes on the floor. I don't like to go to the bathroom when everyone is asleep. It makes me scared in my tummy because I get the pictures in my brain. The ones when the bad man is there and he gets me. Maybe he will jump out and everyone got to be asleep. They won't be able to help me if he is there. The pictures make me scared and shake. I don't stop watching the door. It makes me hold my breath in very tight so I don't have to make a noise.

There are lots of rooms upstairs that he can get to hide in because it is really my Nan's house. There is a bedroom where my Gaga slept. And then there is another that is my Nan's. But my Nan got to be with people to make her better because she is sad about my Gaga being in heaven. She misses him lots. She is going to come back one day. When she is all better. I am excited. I like my Nan at the house.

We all lived in the house when my Gaga got to go to heaven. He got his own room next to mine. I liked to be in there with him. Or in his room downstairs when he didn't make other people better. He talked to people and helped them get better. My Nan says that he hypnotised people. Maybe like a snake did with their funny eyes. He had some ball things. When one bashed down it made them all bash one after the other. He said he used that. I got to play with it as long as I didn't make the strings all tangled. It didn't ever hypnotise me. I got it on the table and me and Mr. Ted looked at it. But we stayed awake the whole time. Maybe it was like magic.

When my Gaga had got to make people better he liked to go for walks. He didn't go far because he was over seventy, he said. He got to be very old. He had a stick and a hat and he walked around the block. It took him a long time to do it. One night when he was going to have a walk. He slipped and falled over on the floor. I got scared and I cried because he didn't be able to get back up again.

I sat and put his head on my legs and then I told him that my Nan is going to get the doctor. He didn't cry like I did when I falled over. But he didn't be able to get back up again. The doctor came to the house. It was the nice doctor. He let me stay with my Gaga and then the ambulance people took him away.

When he came home again he had to stay in bed. He was poorly. My Gaga said his legs got sick and that they is too tired. I liked my Gaga being in bed all the time. The bad man didn't ever get to come because then he would have to get passed my Gaga's room and he didn't ever do that. Maybe he got scared of my Gaga.

At night time I kissed my Gaga night-night all the time. When I did it after he had been in his bed for two weeks. He gave me a big hug and told me to be good. Then I went to bed and my mum came too because she is doing some cleaning things.

My Nan shouted my Gaga and asked if he wanted a cup of tea. But he didn't say yes and she shouted him again. But he didn't hear and then she went to his room and shouted my mum.

My mum locked my bedroom door. I didn't know why. I hadn't been bad. I had been a good boy all the time. I did everything like I was supposed to so the evil didn't come out. I asked Mr. Ted all the time and he said that I was good too. But then my mum locked the door and I didn't know why. I tried to make it open and shout my mum but no one came at all.

It got to dark time. I didn't be scared like always because I knew the bad man couldn't come. But no one came. I got back into bed and went to sleep. In the light time there was no one there too. My mum and dad didn't come to bed. But the door was open and I got out of bed. My Gaga didn't be in his room. But my mum was in the bathroom. She told me that Gaga had died and gone to heaven.

I didn't be sad about it because my Gaga had told me all about heaven. He said it got to be in the sky where the angels lived. Then those angels are people that had gone to heaven and they got to look after all the people in the world. He said when he went to heaven he would look after me. I just got to talk to him, but he wouldn't be able to say words back because angels got invisible.

My mum said I didn't have to go to school. But I wanted to. They got the big lunch time and I got to have lots of food. I didn't cry about my Gaga. He is still there. Just I didn't see him anymore.

## TELLING TEDDY

I went to school. One day when I came home there were lots of people in the house. There were lots of Indian people there too and they talked funny like my Gaga did. They were my mum's brothers. They said they had buried my Gaga. I got sad about that. I wanted to go too and say goodbye to him. I wanted to see what his coffin looked like. Maybe it was like vampires.

My Nan sneaked me to the place on the weekend. I didn't see the coffin. It got put in the ground and then it had all the mud on the top. I didn't be allowed to walk on the grass too. She said that I will make a mess when we got home. Maybe there are monsters under the grass. Like in the story books and then the hands will come up and grab the people and take them into the coffins. Maybe witches got to be there at night. I don't like witches. At school I got to have a teacher. I don't like her. She got a big spot on her nose. I think she is a witch too.

My Nan got sad when we got to where my Gaga is. I told her she didn't have to be sad, but she did it on accident because she missed him lots and lots. We put flowers on the mud and then I looked at the sky and told him goodbye.

# J D STOCKHOLM

## SEVENTEEN

*Mr. Ted. I try to remember everything, but I don't be able to. Maybe I forget to lock the door or to put the keys all the way in and then the bad man comes.*

My mum is still in bed because my brother hasn't got up yet; he is a lazy bones. I don't have to take the medicine before school time because my mum is sleeping and I don't be able to make it myself. I don't get the sore in my tummy while I am at school. I don't like it when my tummy doesn't feel good inside. It makes it hard to sit still at school and then the teacher gets mad because I don't do all my work properly.

My mum makes me take the medicine when I get home instead. She has a new cure from the church. I don't know what it is. She doesn't make it like before with lots of things from the bottle. But she has a bag and it has the powder in it. Then she puts in milk and water and uses my cow cup and tells me to drink it. It is all pink inside.

"It tastes like strawberry milkshake," she says.

But it doesn't taste like the one my Nan gets me. It tastes yucky and makes my throat do the turning thing. Then it wants to come out and the sick is in my throat.

I don't get my sick in the bin. I don't be allowed to get it everywhere. The milkshake is fast and I have to get the sick in my hand or it will get on the floor. I run outside. I am allowed to get it outside. Then my mum doesn't have to clean it all up.

If I get my sick outside I can play outside too. But I play in the alley way that is next to the house and all the way to the other end. I stay near the house because my tummy is too sore and I don't want to play out for very long. It makes me tired and all hot inside. I don't be able to go and lie by the fire because my brother is there first. Sometimes, I sit with Mr. Ted in the corner and we read and be quiet and make stories up.

I wish I could play on my bike, but it hurts to ride it lots of times. I don't be able to sit on the seat or ride very fast. My friends get fed up about it because they have to wait for me all the time. I try to make my legs ride on the bike. But it just hurt lots inside and then I can't stop my eyes from doing the crying.

## TELLING TEDDY

I like to play the ball though. I got it from the alley way. It is like new. All the fur on. It is still nice and yellow and bounces when I chuck it at the wall. Maybe someone lost it.

I play with it and my Nan is in the house. She is seeing my mum. I don't want my Nan to see the sick I did outside so I do it at the back at the bins and then I play with my ball. I don't want my Nan to know that all my badness didn't go away yet. Then maybe she doesn't be able to like me very much.

It is time for my Nan to go home. She comes outside and gives me a hug and a kiss.

"Be a good boy," she says.

She gets her pink lipstick on me like she does lots of times.

I watch my Nan walk away and my dad comes outside. He stands by the back door and smokes a cigarette. He keeps watching me and it makes me scared in my tummy. Maybe I forgot to do something. I got the badness out and I don't know about it. I try to play with my ball. I throw it against the wall at the side of the house and then I catch it. But my eyes keep looking at him. He looks at me and it makes me feel funny inside. Maybe he is going to shout at me.

When his cigarette is all gone he comes into the alley way and stands next to me. I bounce the ball and I make my brain think about other things. Me and Mr. Ted always make sure we do everything right so that we don't get in trouble. Maybe my evil got out and then my badness did something wrong. Maybe he is mad about something I don't know about. Sometimes that got to happen because I don't know the right rule. But I always make sure that I remember next time.

It makes me and Mr. Ted tired sometimes because we don't be able to sleep at night. Maybe my dad is going to shout at me or hit me. I keep playing with my ball but I keep watching my dad. I feel it inside that he is mad at me about something I have done. Sometimes I miss things. But me and Mr. Ted try to do everything right and then there is no badness for me to be shouted at.

When it is dark time me and Mr. Ted watch the door. I tell the bad man and so does Mr. Ted that we are good all day long, but sometimes, he still comes because I am just evil inside.

Sometimes, my dad comes if he doesn't be out with his friends and then he gets to read.

Me and Mr. Ted stay awake when my mum and dad come to bed too. We get to think about all the things we did. Sometimes, the pictures in my brain make me stay awake all night. Mr. Ted doesn't like the pictures. They make us be scared in our tummies but they don't stop. When we get our eyes closed the pictures are back again and there are bad things in them.

We look at the door and at the curtains too. The sun gets his hat on in the light time then the curtains go all orange and make the room lots of nice colours. And then I don't like to go to sleep because it is nearly school time. My mum has shown me how to look at the clock. She says I have to be out of the house by eight thirty or I will be late for school. If I go to sleep in the light time then I won't wake up for the eight thirty time and I will miss school and be bad. So me and Mr. Ted stay up all night long.

I don't want to get late for school because then the teacher will call my mum and I will be in big trouble. I lie in the bed and watch the clock. But I don't like to get out of bed when everyone is sleeping. I lie with Mr. Ted and we let the clock tick until we have to get up at the last minute.

I have to use the bathroom in the mornings. My mum says so. I don't be allowed to use the one outside when it is morning time and everyone is sleeping. My mum says that it makes too much noise when I get the door closed so I have to use the inside one. But I don't like it. It makes me scared. I have to brush my teeth. Use the toilet and then brush my hair. When my dad has used his thing on me at bed time; in the morning I can't go to the toilet very fast. It hurts too bad inside. It means that the bad man can come and get me and that makes me scared. I wish someone in the house will wake up. But they don't if the bad man comes. No one ever hears when I am screaming.

I don't have any breakfast. I am not allowed to make my own. But I don't want to. It is too scary to be downstairs when everyone is upstairs asleep. I am too scared to be in the house. When I get out the bathroom I go down the stairs as fast as I can. It feels like the bad man is behind me. Like he is watching. I have to get outside. I wish I can take Mr. Ted. But I have to leave him at home. I can't breathe until I am outside and in the alley way.

## TELLING TEDDY

I post the key through the letterbox at the front door. I am not allowed to use the front door. Outside, I am safe and the bad man can't ever get me out here. My brain does funny things. It keeps telling me that maybe I didn't lock the back door properly. I have to go in the back yard and check. But it is locked. I push down hard and the door doesn't move. I tell my brain it is locked.

I wish Mr. Ted was here. He would be able to say that it is all locked up. I go in the alley and I walk a little but my brain starts to tell me again that maybe the door isn't locked. I try not to listen. But then it shows me all the pictures of the bad man and maybe he will sneak in and hide. Then he can get me at night time because I didn't lock the door. I go back to the house and check it is locked again.

My brain does it so many times that I cry because I wish it would stop telling me that the door isn't locked. I don't like it. I stand by the door. I press it three times and I tell my brain to see that it is all locked up.

I run to school.

## EIGHTEEN

*Mr. Ted. Why does my badness come out? It comes out and I don't know about it. Then I get told off and my mum and dad don't like me anymore.*

My ball is too noisy.

"Your brother is trying to sleep," my dad says. "He doesn't feel very well and he can't sleep with all your stupid banging."

I don't mean to make lots of noise.

"Why can't you go and play somewhere else?" He asks me.

I don't know. I shrug my shoulders.

"I'm sorry," I say.

I didn't know that it makes lots of noise. I don't be able to hear inside and when other people do it; it doesn't make lots of noise inside. Maybe I do it too hard and then it bangs. I will not ever do it again. I promise.

My dad tells me to give him the ball.

"Where did you get this from?" He asks.

I tell him that I just found it.

"Are you telling the truth?" He asks. "Because I know you like to tell people lies. It's what you do. Just like your Nan. She lies too. You're both deceitful."

I don't know what deceitful is, or how to not be it. I tell the truth all the time. Because the bad man can read minds. Then he knows if I am telling fibs. He would make it hurt if I told lies. I don't ever do it. I tell Mr. Ted everything and then he can tell people for me.

My dad throws my ball over the wall. It goes into the yard at the bottom where it is near the shed and in the dark. I don't like to go down there.

"Don't ever play with a ball at the side of the house again," he says.

I tell him that I won't and that I am very sorry.

My mum is in the kitchen. I can see the light at the window over the top of the wall. I don't want to get my ball back. My dad might tell me off and my mum will get to see me and she will remember I am outside. She will make me come inside and I don't want to because I don't want to go to bed yet. It isn't dark time enough.

If I go near my mum when it is near six then she makes me go in and go to bed. I don't like to. I can hear people playing outside. Then I wish I could to play outside like them.

I wish I could play with Phillip and Anne. But they play lots of things I don't be able to do. So I told them I wasn't playing. Maybe Phillip thinks I don't want to be his friend any more. But I do. I like playing with them. I like playing cops and robbers. When I am on my bike I get to be a cop. I can go the fastest when it doesn't hurt inside.

I play with some lolly sticks on the ground. They are thick and not sticky. Maybe they have been there a long time. Or someone sucked all the lolly off it. I get lollies. My mum lets me get them after school. Only if I am good though. They are just one penny and the lady at the shop makes them all by herself. My mum always lets me have one. Then my throat doesn't be sore.

I dig with the lolly stick in the ground at the bottom of the wall. It is all like mud. It makes my mum mad because she says my dad did it with all his bike things. But I don't know. It is easy to dig in and flick all the stones away. I sit so that my mum isn't able to see me.

I play for a while. Then it gets to dark time. I hear my mum and dad go outside to have their cigarette. Maybe they have all eaten dinner and now they are having the one that they always do when they have eaten. Then they will go and make the dishes clean. Then my brother has his bath time.

I don't say hello to my mum and dad. I don't want them to make me come inside. I don't be scared outside when it is dark time. There isn't anyone that got to hurt me on the outside of the house. But my dad finishes his cigarette and comes into the alley way. He tells me to get into the house because I am all dirty and the bath is ready.

My brother isn't next to the fire. He is sleeping in the bedroom. He has got his bath already. Maybe I have been in my daydreams like I do sometimes and then I don't notice. I don't notice anything when I am having day dreams. Not even if my arms fall off.

I use the bath that my brother has used. We don't have lots of water. My dad says there is just one tank and my mum used it for all her dishes. There isn't lots left.

"Maybe she thinks water is free," he says.

Water is free though. Maybe my dad doesn't know because the water comes from the sky.

I don't like getting in the bath after my brother. All the bubbles are gone and all the warm has gone too. It isn't very deep. I am not allowed to put any more water in. My mum says it doesn't matter. I am just getting all the muck off me and I don't need lots of water to do that. I can do it at the sink with a cloth if I have to. But I am not allowed to get in the bed with all the dirt.

I don't stay in the bath a long time. My mum washes my hair. She says I don't get to do it properly and I leave soap in. Or maybe I don't get the dirt out and because I have blonde hair like my dad then it always looks dirty. She doesn't want people to think we aren't even able to buy soap.

I don't like it when my mum washes my hair. I like it when my dad does it. My mum gets her nails and then she makes it all scratch and hurt. When I say ouch she tells me not to be so soft and then she does it lots harder. Sometimes, I try not to cry when she does it. I cried once. She told me I am like a baby.

My dad is waiting at the top of the stairs when I am all done in the bath. He asks me where my ball is. I tell him that it is in the yard. He says that I should bring my things in at night time if I want to look after them. He says I have to go and get my ball because it might get stolen at the night time.

It is dark and I am going to get my pyjamas on. I tell my dad that I have to be in bed because it is dark time. But he says that I have to go and get the ball first. He says I got it lost and I have to find it. I don't know why he doesn't remember where the ball is. My dad forgets lots of things all the time. But I don't tell him because he gets mad about it when I do. He tells me not to answer him back. I don't know what he means. When I don't answer him back too then he gets mad and hits me.

Maybe my brain is wrong and my dad didn't throw the ball. Sometimes that happens too. It has lots of pictures that are not real. My mum and dad say I make things up because of my imagination. Me and Mr. Ted like the imagination bit. It is where all the stories get to stay. Maybe I put the ball in the yard and I just didn't remember about it. Sometimes my evil gets out and makes me do lots of bad things and I don't know about it.

My mum comes out of the bathroom. She has finished making it all clean again with her cleaning powder. She asks my dad what is wrong. He tells her that I left my ball outside. She says that I have to get dressed and get my slippers on and then I have to go out and get it back. I ask my mum if I can get it in the light time before school. Then I will be able to see it.

My dad says no.

I don't want to go outside. Not the yard at the dark time. It is too dark. It makes my brain think about the pictures of the dark places and all the lots of bad things. It makes me scared inside and I don't want to go outside. It makes me feel like I need to go to the toilet again. But I don't tell my dad. He will make me use the one outside with the dark.

I don't like the back yard. It makes me think about the bad man. One day when I was playing down there. He had been coming to see my mum and then he jumped at the wall and scared me. Maybe he will do it at dark time too and then he will get me and I won't know about it. He made me scared and I screamed and cried. He laughed and he said like my mum did that I am just a big baby. I don't ever go to the bottom of the yard again. Only if my Nan got to be doing her flowers. She likes to make it all pretty.

My dad says that this is why I don't get toys like my brother does. He looks after them and I don't. I leave mine outside all the time.

"If you can't look after something like a ball. Then you don't get to have toys that cost a lot of money," he says.

I put my slippers and my pyjamas on and then I go down to the kitchen and stand by the back door. I open it and look into the dark. Maybe the bad man hides in there and I don't know it. I tell my brain that it is ok. I am not able to hear anyone's feet outside.

My dad is in the kitchen. He crosses his arms and stares at me. He has angry eyes. I look outside. There is some light from the kitchen. But it doesn't get all the way to the bottom. I keep counting to three to make myself go. But I don't count to three four times because then it will be bad. When I got to three. At three times I run into the yard.

I can't look for my ball. My dad shuts the back door and then he turns the kitchen light off and it goes all dark. I cry because I am too scared in my tummy. My sick wants to come out and I want to go to the toilet. Maybe I am going to get my pants wet and then I will get smacked. I squeeze my hands on my arms to make it all go away. It always goes away when I make it hurt on my skin. I do it lots of hard and run to the house.

My dad sits in the chair. He is in the backroom. He asks me where my ball is. I haven't got it. I look at my feet.

"I couldn't find it because you turned off the light," I say.

He hits me in the face and I fall onto the floor.

"Is it my fault?" He asks.

I shake my head. It makes the tears fall off my face.

"The light went off when the door got closed," I tell him. "I don't be able to see in the dark."

My dad digs his hand in my arm and makes me stand up. He smacks me very hard on the leg and I cry really loud.

"Stop it," he says and tells me to go upstairs. "Don't you dare make a noise and wake your brother."

## TELLING TEDDY

### NINETEEN

*Mr. Ted. I'm sorry my mum put you on the floor. I wish you were with me. My mum saw all my badness.*

I get up the stairs to the bedroom my fastest. I don't like to see the dark rooms. I have been bad. Maybe the bad man is hiding in there. I know he isn't in the big bedroom because I can hear my mum in there. She is putting things away. I can hear the drawers open and close. Like when she puts clothes away. I know the bad man isn't there. I can't keep the crying away. It is my fault. I get the badness all the time. I wish that I can get it away. I wish that Mr. Ted knew how to make my evil go away. Maybe he can make me go away too. Then no one gets sad or mad about all the bad things I do.

Maybe I can get the ball in the light time when I go to school. I don't like the back yard in the light time too. But maybe the bad man won't come because it is morning time. Maybe he will wait for me because he knows about my badness. I don't know. But my dad will be mad if I don't get the ball back.

My mum doesn't stay in the bedroom with me. She tells me to get in the bed. She doesn't wait. She gets out of the room and then turns the light off on the landing and makes it all dark. I get scared and get into bed very fast. I don't even be able to check if the bad man is hiding in the room. I check lots of times. Maybe he is there. Maybe all my things aren't away or they aren't in a nice and neat pile. Maybe something isn't good and he is waiting.

I get Mr. Ted and we can't lie down because maybe the bad man will get us and we don't know about it. I get very slow and look at the end of the bed. And then the side. My brain does the pictures thing. I see his smiley face in my brain. I don't like it. Maybe it is going to be there when I look at the side of the bed. But he isn't there. No one is there. But maybe he is behind me when me and Mr. Ted crawled on the side. I am shaking. I can't make it stop. We turn. But there is no bad man at the door.

I lie there and my brain gets lots of bad ideas. Maybe the bad man can hide near the bottom of the bed when me and Mr. Ted didn't look. We were looking over the side of the bed. I am mad with my brain because I have to look and I am scared. If me and Mr. Ted climb to the bottom of the bed; maybe the bad man has sneaked in when we weren't looking and then he crawled around the first side of the bed.

I keep looking and checking and all the time when I don't see him my brain tells me more ideas. Maybe I can read the bad man's thoughts. I lie with Mr. Ted in the middle of the bed. We wish the bad man wasn't there. But I feel him close by. It makes me scared and I want to shout my mum and dad. But they are mad at me.

I stare at the door. The light gets on down the stairs. But it isn't on at the landing. My mum says that it wakes my brother up. But he gets a light in his room because he doesn't like the dark.

I lie with Mr. Ted. We lie there and listen. He lies at the edge. Then if the bad man comes Mr. Ted can make me safe. I hold onto his paw. If I let go then the bad man will come and Mr. Ted will get taken away and maybe I will never see him again.

I listen to everything. I don't let my eyes cry from when my dad hit me. My face stings. It is all hot. But I put the cover at it. Maybe it can go away. My leg hurts too. But it is my fault all the time. Sometimes when my dad hits me, I press it and make it hurt lots more. I am just a stupid bad boy.

I hear the door open for the back room. I listen to the feet. Me and Mr. Ted know everyone's feet in the house. But I never hear the bad man's. But it is my dad's feet coming up the stairs. Me and Mr. Ted hide under the covers. I don't want my dad to be mad at me.

He comes to the bedroom. But he doesn't stand and do his stare thing. I don't like when he does that because it makes me scared about my badness. He gets in the bed next to me. I don't pretend to be asleep anymore. But I don't talk to my dad. I roll over to him and then he get one of the books from the floor.

He put his arm down so I can lie there. I get Mr. Ted and we lie with my dad and he reads. Sometimes he doesn't take all my clothes off. Sometimes he just gets them down.

I don't get time to be pretend for sleep. My dad pulls my clothes down. I hug to him and close my eyes. My dad gets his pants down too. Then he gets me to roll the other way. But he lets me lie on his arm and he still reads the book words to me. I listen to them. Maybe me and Mr. Ted can get far away into one of those pictures. Maybe they help Noddy fix his car because it is broken. Me and Mr. Ted can go there too.

Maybe me and Mr. Ted can go and live in Toyland and then I don't hug Mr. Ted up to my face. I don't want my dad to be mad that I cry again. He always tells me not to cry. Just like a big baby. I am always crying. Maybe I am not a real boy to cry so much. Maybe like a sissy girl he says.

I hear the door downstairs get open again. The one for the back room. It makes a pop when it gets open. It never gets opened quiet. I hear my mum's feet get fast up the stairs and then my dad pulls my clothes up and his own pants. But he doesn't do it properly and I have to. He reads the book again.

My mum comes into the room. She looks very mad. She gets her angry face. She gets the covers like the bad man does. She pulls them hard and fast off the bed. They get away fast and I am not able to catch them. She asks me and my dad what we are doing. He tells her we are reading because I am upset about the ball. She asks him to come downstairs so they can turn everything off and go to bed.

She goes back downstairs and my dad goes too. It is very late I think. I don't know. I can't see the clock in the dark time. I hear the door again and my mum put the big chain on the front door. She does that at bed time. Then no robbers get in the house.

Then she comes upstairs and she put the lamp on. She gets her bed things on and gets in bed. She tells me to move to the middle. She has one of my books with her. Not the same book. I want to ask if she can read it to me. But maybe she is mad.

"Do you feel better?" She asks.

I nod my head.

"Yes."

I wish to Mr. Ted in secret that I don't want my mum to go back downstairs. I want her to stay upstairs. So I can go to sleep and no one can hurt me. My mum doesn't go to bed early. She likes it late because she watches the television with the scary things on it.

My dad comes upstairs too. I hear him turn off the lights in the hallway and then he comes up the stairs. It makes me feel happy inside. I can go to sleep and no one can hurt me. Me and

Mr. Ted hug in the middle. We are all squashed so I am not in the way and then my dad doesn't tell me to sleep on the box.

My dad gets into bed. They talk about boring things and they laugh. I close my eyes. I like being there. Then the bad man doesn't get me.

My dad doesn't have any clothes on. He has taken them off to get in bed. My mum gets the cover and makes it slid down the bed. It is cold. I don't know why she pushes it down. She gets my hand and then she puts it behind me on my dad's thing.

She tells me to hold it and then to move my hand. It isn't like when my dad does it. He holds my hand for me. My mum tells me what to do and I get the scared feeling in my tummy. I try to pretend to go to sleep. But she is talking to me. She takes Mr. Ted and puts him on the floor next to her. My eyes let some of the tears out. But not lots of them. I want Mr. Ted.

My mum keeps telling me to make my hand move. She starts to pull my pyjama top up and then she takes it off. She does it with my pants too. I lifted myself up so she can get them down and she pulls them all the way off so I don't have any clothes too.

My mum tells me to let go of my dad's thing. He is reading the book to me. My mum pushes me and I slide on the bed to my dad and then he put his thing inside and my mum is here and she looks at it. I wish she would look away. She lies with us. My dad doesn't hurt me like he does when I get bad. Just the little hurt when we can read. But I don't like it. I don't want my mum to see. She can see how bad I am. The evil gets me to do these things with my dad. I am very bad. Maybe the bad man will come too.

# TELLING TEDDY

## TWENTY

*Mr. Ted. I can't make it all clean again. Now I be bad on the outside too.*

I want to ask Mr. Ted if my evil got too big. My mum doesn't give me the medicine in the morning times anymore and I don't get all the sick from my tummy at the day time. Maybe my badness got out too much and now my dad needs help to get rid of it. I am just an evil boy like my mum says. Maybe I will always be evil. I wish that I am good like people at school. They get to be good and then other children like them. They get nice things like new toys and clothes. They get all the good things at school. I am just stinky and bad all the time. No one ever likes me because of the evilness. Maybe they can see it all the time. I wish it would go away. Maybe I will never ever get better.

It makes me sad in my tummy when the other children at school all get hugs and kisses from their mums and dads. I don't know how they get to be so good. Even the ones that are bad at school are always good. I wish I am good like Phillip and Anne. They don't ever get shouted at. Their dad doesn't hit them and they don't ever get the bad man. I don't tell them about the bad man for me though. Maybe they wouldn't want to be my friend any more.

Phillip and Anne don't have evil parts. Maybe when I get to be like them I will be better and I will get nice things. They have nice things. They have lots of toys and new bikes. They even got on an aeroplane and went somewhere all sunny. It had a big swimming pool. Phillip said it was giant and they had lots of things to play on. I wish one day I will get to go on holiday. Maybe when I am better I can go with my mum and dad and my brother and then we will do all the nice things together. Maybe my mum and dad will like me and be my friend if I am good inside.

My dad stops the hurt thing. My mum tells me that I have to go and use the toilet. She gives me my pyjamas back. She says I have to put them on too. But I am not allowed to until I have been to the toilet. I have to make sure that I make my hands all clean and turn the light off.

It is dark in the hallway. There aren't lights on very much. I can see the dark downstairs. I don't like looking down there. Maybe the bad man is hiding at the top and then will jump out.

I don't like to walk to the bathroom. I know there is no bad man. But I still feel the scared inside my tummy. I get the pictures in my brain that he will jump out and get me.

I don't hear the bad man in the house. My dad has already done the hurt thing so the bad man doesn't need to make me hurt too. I haven't been lots of bad. I just got my ball lost. Maybe I will find it and then it will all be better in the morning and my mum doesn't have to see the hurt part for my badness.

I go to the bathroom my fastest. I turn the light on. There is no bad man. I check everywhere and I push the door closed so he can't get in the bathroom with me. Or get his hand at the door and turn the light off. Maybe he is hiding until my mum and dad fall to sleep. Maybe they fall to sleep while I am in the bathroom and then he can get me and they won't hear me when I shout them.

I use the toilet like my mum told me to do. I do it just right. I watch the door and then the bad man can't come in and I don't be too long. I get my clothes on. I have to put my pants on first. That's what my mum says and then my top. I have to do it just right like she says and then I don't get told off.

I feel all the bad inside. I wash my hands, but they don't feel good. I can feel all my evil on my skin. It makes my hands feel bad. I wish I can take them off for new clean hands. Mine are dirty and bad. I feel like lots of creatures on them. I wish I could have a bath. Then I could get them all washed away.

I wash my hands. I do them hard. I make the soap get everywhere and then it gets all the evil. I rub them three times on the front and three times on the back. I get them all dry again. They still feel bad inside. I am bad. I want to go to the bedroom and get in the bed with my mum and dad. I don't want my mum and dad to fall to sleep and then the bad man can get me.

I have to wash my hands again. I get the soap between all the fingers and all over my hands like before. I do it all the same. I rub it lots and lots of times so it is all big giant bubbles. Then I put my hands under the water, but the water is very hot. I put my hands in there to wash the badness away. Maybe the hot can make it go away.

It won't go away. My brain keeps saying they are still bad. I have to wash them again and again. They are still dirty. The badness is still inside them. I want it to go away. I can only wash them one more time. I have to make them clean properly.

I get my hands all soapy again. I do it slow and I put them in the hot water. They hurt, but that is good. It makes the badness go. They have to get hurt to get better. And if I do it slow. Then I know when they are right. Then the badness doesn't feel so bad. It makes the crying be there behind my eyes. I got the soap all off again. But my badness isn't gone. It is there. All over.

I make my fingers dig into my arms. Maybe I can get the badness to scare away. Maybe I can make it come out and go away. I dig hard. I dig and let it make my eyes cry. I look at the mirror. I wish I could hit my face. Maybe my dad can do it and then the badness will leave.

I get away from the sink. I don't want to look at the mirror. I see my badness there. It is all inside. That is why they do all the bad things to me. I am evil inside. I can see it in the mirror. I wish I could go away forever. Then I won't make my mum and dad so mad all the time. They will get to do nice things. Maybe my brother won't get sick all the time too.

I turn the light off and I have to walk to the bedroom. I do it slow. Then the bad man can get me. Then he can hurt me and he can make it hurt very bad. That's what happens when I am bad. I have to get the hurt part. I have been very bad. I got my dad to do those things and my mum was there. Maybe the bad man can hit me too.

The bad man doesn't get me though. He isn't there. Or maybe he just doesn't want to because I am too bad. Maybe even he doesn't like me anymore.

I go to the bedroom. My mum and dad are in bed. My mum lets me get in the bed. But I have to sleep at the edge. Maybe I should sleep on the box instead. So then I can get all cold. I don't have a bed because bad boys don't get nice things.

I don't let my eyes close all night long. I wait for the bad man to come. He is going to. I know he is there. He is hiding somewhere. I feel him watching. I watch the door all night. But he doesn't come.

# J D STOCKHOLM

## TWENTY ONE

*It's my birthday today Mr. Ted. I am seven.*

I don't think the bad man has to come anymore because my mum is there to see my badness. Maybe she told him I am good. If I do the things she says then that is being good. I let my dad do the things to me. I do what my mum says when she tells me to. We do it like that lots of times. I haven't seen the bad man again. I let my dad do all the hurt parts and my mum is there.

I don't like it when she sees all the bad things I do. I don't like it when she tells me to put his thing in my mouth. She tells my dad to do things too at the same time. They hurt too, but we both do as we are told.

My birthday is always in the school holidays. It is just before the Halloween time. I wish that my birthday got to be on Halloween. Then I would be able to have ghosts and scary things. If I ever got a birthday. I don't have one yet. Not real ones. Not like my brother does or my friends. I don't mind. Me and Mr. Ted talk about it.

I am going to be seven. I make myself be good all the time. That's why I don't get the birthdays. Because I am never good. My mum says when I don't listen to the devil anymore then I can get a big party.

I don't tell people about my birthday. Sometimes it makes me sad inside. I don't know how to get the evil gone so I can have one. I wish I could get presents. Maybe this time my mum would see how good I have been.

I don't ask my mum for things all the time. I go out to go and play. My mum says I can go out in the morning. But I am not allowed to make lots of noise. My dad says if I wake my brother up then there will be really big trouble and I will pay for it.

"You'll have to get your brother settled and back to sleep," he says.

I go to play outside with Phillip and Anne. I stay out all day long because I don't want my mum to make me come inside. She makes me go to bed. Even if it is still light time. When I go to bed like that the bad man might come back and I don't like it. So I stay outside.

Me and Phillip and Anne are playing out on the bikes. We have some other friends too. There is one called Ben. He lives around the corner. He just lives in one room with his mum. They don't have lots of money and my mum doesn't really like me to play with him because she says his mum is just a fat blob. I think his mum is nice. She lets me play with Ben's He-man cat. I wish I had my own Battlecat. I ask Mr. Ted if he can ask for one for my birthday. Or maybe Santa can get me one. Only if I am good though. Maybe I will be all growed up before I get a Battlecat.

We also have a friend called Damien and one called Lawrence. And there is a girl called Kirsty. She doesn't get to play lots of times. She is my girlfriend. But only in the school time and it is a secret. She is new at the school. But her dad is very busy and they have a big hotel. She has to help do the work there. But we call for her too and she comes out and plays.

Ben lives on a road that is near to school and near my dad's work too. But it is a nice road and we can race bikes and skates on it. It doesn't get filled with lots of bumps and then it has a big slope at the end. We have to be careful though. There is a crazy dog there. He is called Snoopy. He doesn't look like Snoopy and he doesn't sleep on top of his house. He is little and black and mean. He likes to bite people if they got too fast.

Me and Ben are on skates. We are having a race. We have raced all of us. But now it is just me and Ben because we are the fastest and then we need to see who the winner is. The loser has to go and run past Snoopy.

I try my best. But Ben is bigger than me and he wins. But I'm too tired and it is hard to breath. My Nan says it is called out of puff. But I have to find Snoopy and we have to race him too. Maybe he will catch me and eat me all up.

Damien says that he knows where he lives and that we should go there. So we do. We all follow Damien. It is just at the other road near Ben's road. Snoopy lives in a big green house. It has a garden like a big jungle. He tries to look but Snoopy isn't in the garden. There is an old man though. He is very old. Maybe like one of those old beggar people that walked with crooked legs.

"What are you doing?" He asks.

Damien says that we have been racing.

"Who won?"

Ben tells him that he did. He asks if we all like to play snooker. I have never got to play it before. But I have seen it on the television. I don't know what to do though. But I still say yes. The old man says that he has a table inside and maybe we would like to go in and play with it.

We all do.

Snoopy is in the house. He is in his bed. Not a house like the real Snoopy. He doesn't get up and be mean to us. We go to the backroom of the house. It is full of lots of things and smells like old people.

We play snooker and the man gives us lemonade to drink. It is fizzy and makes the bubbles go up my nose. But I like it a lot. He says if we take the empty bottles to the shop for him, then we can keep the money from them. He has lots of them. There are three bottles each.

I don't know what the rules are for the snooker. But the man has lots of books. He has a giant shelf with millions of books. Maybe he has his own library. There are so many of them. I look at them.

"Do you like to read?" He asks.

"Yes," I say and I make my head nod and tell him about all the books I read. He likes them too. He says his eyes don't get so well anymore so he can't read. I tell him I can read. He thinks the books are too hard for me.

They aren't. I can read all the books. I show him. He says I can read really good. He says that I can come back and read and then I can take the bottles with me and that can be my money. I like that very much. I tell him yes please.

It is late and we all have to go home again. We say goodbye and I say thank you.

I go to the old man's house every day. All of us do. He likes to let us play and then I read books too. It is very nice of him to let us be there. Sometimes he asks us to go to the shop and get him things. We always do because he is always good and sometimes he says we can keep the change.

I have enough money to get some chips at the shop. Then I can eat them before I go home and my tummy isn't hurting lots because I don't get dinner.

## TELLING TEDDY

It is the last day of the holiday. It is going to be my birthday in the morning. I am excited inside. I have been very good all the time. My mum and dad haven't had to shout at me. And at the night time my dad reads the books to me and my brother and I don't ever cry at the things he got to do. I do what he says and what my mum says. I try my bestest. I tell Mr. Ted. He thinks I have been very good too.

I hug him. I wish that in the morning I will get a Battlecat.

It is light time. I lie all awake. I am awake before the sun comes out. I wish I could make my mum and dad wake up and then they might give me a present. I lie still and me and Mr. Ted watch the sunshine and the clock. It takes forever for my mum and dad to wake up.

It is to be Saturday. My dad goes to the library on Saturday. Maybe he will take me too for my birthday. I wish that I can have a cake too.

My mum and dad wake up. They don't say anything. My dad gets out of his bed and then he smokes a cigarette and gets dressed.

My mum tells me to get up and get dressed. We all go downstairs. Maybe my presents are there. But she tells me to come in the kitchen and she gives me my yucky milkshake medicine. It makes the sick come from my tummy and I don't have any sick because I haven't eaten any breakfast. It makes my throat all sore inside.

I get the sick all out and go into the backroom. I sit and wait. I don't see any presents. Maybe they hid them. They do for my brother and then my dad pretends that they forgot and my brother pretends to get sad.

They don't give me anything. My dad goes out to the library. I don't go with him. I ask my mum if I can go out and play. She says that I can. I go to the old man's house. But I don't want to play with the snooker or read the books. The old man asks me what is wrong. I make my shoulders shrug. I don't tell him I am evil inside and I don't get birthdays.

I play all day, but I don't stay till dark time at the man's house. Maybe my mum will make me a birthday tea like she does for my brother. Maybe they have a surprise for me. I go home.

But the dinner is already gone and my mum is making the dishes all clean.

My dad is at the table. He has his special drink. I ask him if it is my birthday today. He puts his paper down and says yes it is. He tells me that it is hard to get things for birthdays.

"We don't have a lot of money," he says. "And you don't look after your toys very well anyway, so you don't need anymore."

He is right. He talks lots that I don't need toys anymore. All my friends don't have toys because now we are all too big and when he was seven he didn't have toys too. He says that he just read books.

He says that boys don't need lots of toys because they have an imagination. Children with toys just make lots of noise and mess and then my mum has more things to clean up. He says that toys cost too much money and he doesn't have lots of work to do to make lots of money. He tells me that when he gets more work then we can waste money on lots of things like new toys and new clothes.

I can't stop the crying in my eyes. I don't let my dad see. I make my mouth open like a yawn and then he doesn't see the wet on my face. I ask my dad if I can sit on the floor and play with my cars. My dad says that I can. But I have to make it all tidy again when I am done because my mum has just got everything cleaned up. I say I will. I sit with my car and my Larry the lamb and Mr. Ted. The tears keep falling off my face and making my leg wet. I keep making them wipe away.

My dad asks if I would like to go upstairs and read.

I say yes.

## TELLING TEDDY

### TWENTY TWO

*Mr. Ted. I am too bad. The police have got to take me to jail like a bad robber.*

I don't remember my mum telling me no one is going to be home. No one had told me. Maybe I don't remember. I am home from school and there is no one here. Maybe they have just gone out. But the car isn't here too. I knock on the back door. But no one answers. My mum doesn't lock it in the day time. It just open, but I try it. It doesn't move and I don't be able to see her in the kitchen.

My mum is always in the kitchen. She is always very busy in the light time. She has lots of things to do to look after everyone in the house. We make a mess all the time. And my brother is sleepy all the time. She has to do lots of things to look after him she says.

I look in the back window. There is no one there too. The television isn't on and my brother isn't by the fire.

I am not allowed to use the front door. But I go around to it. It has a doorbell and maybe everyone is upstairs and they don't hear me at the back door. I open the letter box and look inside. But it is all dark in there. I don't look for long., Maybe I will see the bad man in the house. Maybe he is up the stairs and waits until later.

He will be mad because I am at the front door. My mum will get mad if I am home late from school. She will shout and ask me why I am late and what I was doing. I have to go straight home. She doesn't come and get me from school anymore because she is too tired to do it. I go to school all by myself so I am big enough to get home too.

I wish I had a coat. I just went in my school jumper and a shirt. My coat is too small for me. I have grown too much and my mum doesn't have the money to get a new one yet. I wish they get some soon because it is nearly winter time. Soon we will get all the big winds. My Nan says they are called gales. All the big trees don't have any leaves on them anymore. I hope I get a new coat soon. Before I get all frozen and turned into an icicle.

I have to sit outside. I try to sit in the alleyway. But it is too wet and the rain is cold. It gets through my clothes and makes me shiver. My teeth shake together and then my fingers and toes are all stinging because they are cold too. My mum is going to get mad because my clothes are all wet. She says the rain is dirty. She doesn't like rain on clothes. Then she has to wash them and it is more work for her and she never ever gets to sit down. My mum will get all mad. She will shout at me and then my dad will get mad too and maybe he will hit me for it. Then at bed time he will do the hurt thing. I don't like to be bad. But I don't know how to make the rain get off my clothes.

Maybe when they get home I can get my dad to do the hurt thing. I do that. Then he doesn't need to. I already know when I am bad. So I get my dad to do it. I don't want my mum to tell him. I tell Mr. Ted about it. He thinks it is right too. Then I get my books and go to my dad and ask him to read. Then he does the thing all the time. Sometimes he doesn't make it hurt. But he is supposed to.

I go in the back yard. I know that I am not allowed in my dad's shed. But I know where he keeps the key. It is in the toilet room outside. I don't like to go down there. I don't like the yard. It is scary when there is no one in the house too. Maybe the bad man will hide somewhere and then no one will ever come.

It is quick to go there. I tell my brain that I can run and get it. I am very cold. My hands shake all the time. I look down the yard. I can see all the way. There is no one there. I have the scared feeling on my back. It makes me feel like there is someone there. My brain tries to tell me things. They get me all scared inside. I can see lots of pictures. It makes things up sometimes. It has pictures about the forest and people. They all did bad things. The flowers at the garden made my brain make these pictures.

The pictures have flowers that is the same. They are roses. My Nan likes roses very much. But they make me think of the building with the roses outside the window. I don't like that place. They eat little boys and girls in there and feed them to monsters.

I get the shed unlocked. I can feel the badness inside. I don't know if I should go in there. But I am so cold. Even my ears are sore and I don't have a hat. It is dry in there. I don't know why I don't be allowed in the shed. It just has lots of motorbike bits and my dad's big giant bike. He has magazines and newspapers and some cans from his beer that he drinks with his friends. And then a bottle of his special whiskey drink.

I go inside the shed and then I close it behind me. I keep the key in my pocket. I wish I had Mr. Ted. Then he could help me listen to the house. I want to listen so I know when my mum and dad came back. Before they see me and then they get all mad about it.

I don't touch anything in the shed. I try not to look at anything too. My dad says I don't be allowed to look at his things. I am not good enough. Maybe I will get my evilness on them. I look at the floor and not my dad's things. I sit on the magazines because I don't want to get his chair all wet. Then he will be mad about that. The magazines are next to the window.

The window makes a little bit of light. I don't want to put the big light on for the shed. Then my dad will get mad at using all the power. But I hold my book up then I can read the words and I can to read it.

It starts to get dark. I don't be able to see in the dark. Not like rabbits. Maybe if I eat lots of carrots like they do I can see in the dark. But I don't. So I put my book in my bag. My mum and dad are still not home. My tummy hurts because I am hungry. I don't get dinner. But sometimes I got to steal things off the plates. It makes the tummy ache go away. And the medicine my mum got me to have makes me not be hungry too. It just makes me get the sick out. But there is no medicine in the shed.

I wish I knew where my mum and dad have gone to. I don't remember them saying that they are going out. Maybe they did and I didn't listen. My mum says I don't listen all the time. That's why I get into trouble so much. I am too busy being bad and not listening that I never do anything right.

I need to use the toilet. But I am scared in my tummy about that too. The outside toilet is next to the shed. I know there is no bad man in there. Unless he got to sneak in when I am reading and then I didn't hear him. But I have to look in the yard. It is dark and maybe the bad man is hiding there. My brain keeps making me look at the window. Maybe the bad man will sneak up and then he will get me.

I don't want to go outside all by myself. I wish my mum and dad would come home very soon and then I can go to bed and go to the toilet. My dad can read to me because I am bad and then I can go to sleep and be warm. My dad will get very mad if I got to the toilet in his shed. Maybe he will just hit me forever and ever.

I hug my arms and lean on the wall. It is cold too. It makes my cold clothes stick on me. My eyes are tired and they feel like there is fire in them. I close them. Only for a little bit. I don't want the bad man to sneak in. I make my ears listen to all the noises. Maybe I can sleep with my eyes open.

I don't hear anyone come in the shed. I don't even hear my mum and dad come home. Maybe I have gone to sleep. I don't remember that. My clothes are still a little wet and I am a stick and frozen.

My dad hits me across the face with the back of his hand. I don't get to catch myself because I don't know he is there. I fall on the floor. It makes me hurt because the floor is hard and I bang my head and squash my arm.

My dad kneels down next to me. He gets my clothes and makes me lift up. He hits me again and my nose starts to bleed. I don't want to get it on my clothes. I am sorry for breaking into his shed. I know I am bad. I should have stayed outside. I didn't mean to fall to sleep. I don't mean to make them mad. I wish I could go away.

"Now I have to call the police," he says. "I don't have any other choice."

He will get everyone in trouble if he doesn't. I have done a bad thing. I have broken in like a robber. If he doesn't tell then he will get in trouble and everyone will have to go to jail. Even my brother. I don't want him to go to jail.

My dad drops me on the floor again. Then he walks out of the shed to telephone the police. They have to take me away and put me in jail like all the bad robbers.

## TELLING TEDDY

### TWENTY THREE

*Mr. Ted. Please tell my dad not to hit me. I am sorry.*

I don't want my dad to call the police. I don't want them to come and take me away. I don't want to go to jail and not see my mum and dad again. My Nan will be mad at me if I go to jail. Maybe she will never be my friend again. She doesn't like robbers and bad people. She has a friend who had a robber. She wishes the robber will get caught and then get in big trouble. Maybe my Nan will wish I get in big trouble too.

I don't make anything go away. Not like a real robber. I don't break things or steal them. I just did the break in part. I want to tell my dad that I am sorry. I get off the floor and I run to him. He is in the house. In the kitchen.

My mum is going to get mad at me because I got blood off my nose on my school uniform. She doesn't like when it got dirty. Some got all over my hands and on my sleeve. It makes my shirt get red. I don't mean to be so bad. Everyone will be mad at me.

My dad asks me what I am doing. I tell him that I am sorry. I don't know how to make my sorry very strong. I shout it at him lots of times. He just stands there because he doesn't hear me properly. I say it lots and lots of times.

"I don't have a choice," he says. "The rest of the family will get into trouble. "

I try to stand in the way so then my dad can't get to the backroom where the telephone is. But my dad pushes me out of the way. I am very scared inside. I don't want to go to jail. I don't want the police to come and take me away. I will never see anyone ever again. It makes my tummy and everything inside all squeezed together.

I grab my dad's hand. I don't let go because I don't want him to go and use the telephone. He gets mad at me and goes in the backroom. I use both my hands to hold his and then he can't get the telephone. He has big hands. They are all big and strong. He gets my hand and pushes the little finger back. I don't be able to get my hand out of his. He does it and my hand feels like it is going to fall off into a million pieces all on the floor. I cry very loud because it hurts so bad. But he doesn't let it go.

My dad tells me that I have to go upstairs. I ask him not to call the police.

"I have to," he says.

But he will do it in the morning because they are closed. I don't believe him. He is going to do it when I go out the room and I don't want him to. Then they will get me.

"I'm glad you didn't come with us today," my dad says.

My brother is crying and my mum puts him on her knee.

"Look at what you did with all your noise. I'm glad you didn't come because you would have ruined the day."

They had gone out to buy new things and I didn't get any because I don't ever behave.

I keep telling him I am sorry. I don't mean to be bad all the time. Just the evil does it and then I don't notice to make it stop.

I cry for him to let my hand go. But he doesn't do it. He makes my fingers all go back. He pushes them very hard. He puts his face close to mine and then I have to get on the floor with my knees. He shouts very loud. My brother cries lots more because I am bad. I don't like it when my dad shouts very loud. It makes me very scared inside and then my ears all hurt.

I don't be able to stop it. My pants get all wet. My dad tells me that I am a baby. He laughs because I have wet my pants. He tells me to go upstairs and stay there I am not allowed to get new clothes on.

"Don't want you pissing up all your clean clothes," he says.

My dad drags me to the door and makes me go to the hallway. He pushes me. But I don't want to go. He is going to call the police. But my dad puts me in the hall in the dark. He shouts to get all the way in the bedroom. I don't get allowed to put the lights on. He pushes me out and then he closes the door. I try to make it get open. But my dad pushes it on the other side.

"Get up the damn stairs right now," he yells at me.

My tummy gets the shakes inside. Maybe it is like the bats. Maybe they are all sad inside them. I don't get to stop my teeth from banging together and I have the hiccups too. My head wants to go pop like a balloon. I go up the stairs. But I squeeze myself altogether. Then the bad man isn't able to reach me and drag me into a room in the dark.

I go to the bedroom. It is dark in there too. I don't want to go in. maybe the bad man is hiding on the other side of the bed.

I hear the door downstairs get open. Then the lights go on and then I hear my dad's feet on the stairs. He is running very fast. My dad gets to the top of the stairs. He has his angry face. He is very mad at me. He runs to me and I get in the bedroom. I put my hands up. He is going to hit me. I put my hands there so then he can't smack me. I tell him I am very sorry. I don't get in the bedroom right away.

My dad pushes me back and I fall over in the room. He says that I don't get to do things right. All he had done was tell me to go to the bedroom and I didn't do that. I can't help it. It is my badness. I am sorry. I wish I am like all my friends. They are all good and they all don't get shouted at. I am so bad. I am very bad inside. I can feel it there. I wish I could make it get out and go away.

My dad closes the bedroom door. Then he locks it and leaves me in there. Mr. Ted is in the bed. I pick him up and hug him very tight. I wish he got big arms then he can hug me back. It is all dark inside. I walk at the wall in case the bad man is hiding under the bed. He isn't at the other side of the bed. There is no one there.

I go to the box with Mr. Ted and we open the window a little bit and then the curtain. There is a light outside and it makes some of the dark go away. Me and Mr. Ted look at the door and we see if the bad man got in the room when we don't know about it. We stare and keep looking all the time in case he is there.

We stay there a long time. Then I hear the door for the backroom. Then I hear my dad come up the stairs. I don't know what he is doing. I close the window and the curtain. He doesn't like it to be open. He says I let all the heat go out and he isn't heating the damn street. But he uses bad words when he says it.

I stand in the corner. My dad is at the other side of the door. Maybe he is waiting for the bad man. I can see his feet at the door in the light. I don't move. I stand very still like a statue. I squash myself at the wall with Mr. Ted. My eyes keep leaking because I know my dad is going to come and shout at me again. I can feel all the sick in my tummy. It mixes around.

My dad opens the door and he stares at me and Mr. Ted. He doesn't have his angry face. He looks at me. I don't look at him. I look at my feet. I can feel the badness and my dad is looking at it. My dad comes to me and Mr. Ted. He moves me to the box and makes me sit down. He puts his hand on my face. He is going to hit me. But he doesn't. His hand gives my face a hug.

My dad puts my head back. He tells me to close my eyes. I do. I hear his pants open. But he doesn't make mine open and he doesn't take them off. He tells me to open my mouth and then he put his thing there.  I don't have my book. My dad doesn't read to me. He always reads to me. Then I can hear the book words. But he doesn't. He gets me to do that thing to him and it makes my throat want to be sick when he gets to the end.

My dad tells me to go to the bathroom and brush my teeth. I have to be very fast and then sit on the box and not move.

I get to the bathroom. I get my teeth all clean. I clean them lots of times because my mouth is all bad inside. I get the water in my hands and then make it wash my mouth. But then on accident I swallow some water. It makes my tummy feel very thirsty. I make my hand into a cup because I don't have one and then I drink lots of water.

My dad shouts at me to hurry up. But I don't be able to stop drinking the water. Maybe I will drink it all. I shout at myself in my brain to stop it. I am very bad.

I go back in the bedroom. I sit on the box. I stay there all night long.

## TELLING TEDDY

### TWENTY FOUR

*I was a robber today Mr. Ted. I am very sorry. I know the bad man will come.*

I am so hungry. It makes my tummy hurt really bad. In my brain I think about all the food like breakfast. My mouth pretends it is there too. I can pretend what it tastes like. It is yummy. It makes my mouth get thirsty. My tummy makes a hurt sound. Like big monsters growling. It doesn't like not having any food inside. But I am not allowed anything. I have not been very good. Because I am so bad all the time. Then I can't have dinner and I can't have breakfast. Robbers don't get food but the police aren't going to come. My dad has called them and told them that I won't do it ever again. I am happy that the police aren't going to come. I am not a real robber. Robbers only make messes and got in houses at the night time when everyone is sleeping.

Maybe I can be a food robber. At school yesterday. I got to eat chicken pie and mashed potatoes. It makes my tummy jump up and down when I think about it. It tasted very nice. I also got chocolate pudding with chocolate custard. I wish I had some more. It is my favourite. Mr. Ted likes it too. We write all about it in our book. When I am big, I am going to eat it all the time. It makes my tummy very hungry when I think about all the food at school. It is going to take ages and ages to be lunch time again.

It is a very long time until it is school time. The sun has just got up. It woke me up because I had sleeped on the box all night long. My head fell to sleep then I got woke up because it falled over and made me jump. I don't get to lie on the box. Not when I am wearing stinky wet clothes. I lean on the wall.

I don't remember the going to sleep part. I was awake when my mum and dad got to bed. I watched at the door all night and then the bad man didn't come. Then my eyes had got all sleepy and gone to sleep by themselves. I didn't know about it. Sometimes that happens. I get very tired when I have lots of days awake and then my brain just makes me go to sleep all the time.

It happens lots of times when my dad is reading to me and my brother. Sometimes I fall asleep. I don't mean to. I just do it on pretend. But then the sleep comes and I go to real sleep. I don't like it because then when I wake up all my clothes is gone. My brother be sleeping too. He still has his clothes on and he is asleep on the pillows. Then my dad has got all my clothes off and all of his and then his thing is already inside. It makes me wake up because it hurts.

I don't like it because then the hurt part feels like it is in my dreams. When I wake up for real I feel all my badness inside. I wish I can take it away. I don't want my dad to know about my badness. I don't tell him that I am really awake. But I always ask him if I can go to the bathroom after. I pretend that I just woke up. I wish that my dad never got to know how bad I am.

Sometimes, I wish I don't wake up ever. It feels like there is a big monster inside. My mum says that is when I can feel the devil inside. I don't know how to make him go away. I try to scratch at my skin. But that doesn't make him go away. Sometimes, I get my hands and then I hit myself very hard. But that doesn't take him away. He hides inside forever. My mum's medicine doesn't make him go away too.

My dad wakes up because I look out of the window. I make the curtain move and it makes the sun go on his eyes. The milk man is outside. He is in his milk cart. Then he puts all the new milk on all the doorsteps for when the people all get out of bed. We don't get milk on our doorstep. My mum says we have to pay and then it is a waste of money.

I wish I had money. Because the milkman has things on his cart that people can go and buy. But I don't have any left. I had some more from the old man when I took his bottles back. But I have spent it all on chips when it was Sunday. Then I ate them all by myself and I don't have any money left.

My dad shouts at me to shut the curtain.

"If you are awake then go to school," he says.

But it isn't the school time yet. The clock doesn't say it is eight. It is only at six. There is no school open for ages and ages.

I tell my dad that it isn't school time. He says he doesn't care. He tells me not to bother getting changed.

"You can go as you are," he says. "If you can't behave then you don't deserve to get changed."

I still have my uniform on. It isn't wet any more. The pants have all got dry at the night time when I was on the box asleep. I don't go to the bathroom though. I am bad and maybe then the bad man is hiding. I go out of the house my fastest. I lock the door and I tell myself that it is all locked. My brain always does the no it isn't thing.

I put the keys in the letterbox and see the milk man is still on the road. So is the paper boy. I watch them and then my brain tells me to go and check the door again. It makes me mad because it doesn't shut up. I wish it did. But it keeps telling me the door isn't locked. I go to the back and I push the handle. I tell my brain out loud.

"The door is locked."

I don't use the alley way to go to school. I don't want to go right there. Maybe I can get lost. I wonder if I can. But I know all the streets. Maybe if I walk I can go and not know where I am. I walk out of the street and I tell my brain to stop it about the door. It makes me not want to walk. I look at the house and then I get mad because I tell my brain one more time.

I walk back to the main street. It is all quiet. There isn't anyone walking around. Even the milkman has not got the milk there yet. The houses have lots of empty bottles at the door steps. They get changed for new ones. But he doesn't do it yet. One of the bottles has a note inside. There is money on the step next to the bottle. I stand at the gate and look at it. It is lots of money.

It makes my heart do the jumpy thing inside. Like it does when my dad is going to come and shout at me. I look all over the street. I look at the house. All the curtains are closed. The houses on the sides are all asleep too. There is no one looking. I am all hot inside. And then I don't know how to breathe right. It makes me feel like I have been running all about.

I stand there and count. One, two, three. Then I run in the garden. I get the money and I run my fastest all the way down the big road. I know there is someone there. They have seen me and I feel them chasing behind me. They will shout at me and tell my mum and my dad. Then the bad man will come because I am bad and stole some money. I am like a real robber. I run all the way to the park. My legs don't want to run anymore. I get inside and then I hide behind a bush. Maybe I can get away.

I feel like a big bad robber. I have to hide in the bushes and then I can listen for anyone running. But I don't hear anyone. Maybe I got away. I did run very fast. I look out at the big road.

But there isn't anyone there. I am all alone. I sit on the ground. I have the money in my hand. It is lots of money. I feel all bad inside. Maybe the people at the house don't have lots of money. Maybe I can give them some more back when I have got some.

## TELLING TEDDY

### TWENTY FIVE

*I got to play on the park today all by myself. Then I was good. But maybe the bad man will come because I spended the stolen money. I'm sorry Mr. Ted.*

There is another big road near the park. I have been to it sometimes. It is where the dentist lives. I don't like the dentist. He always makes me go to sleep with the stinky gas stuff. Then I get sick in my tummy and my mum gets mad because I walk home too slow.

But there is a shop next to it. Sometimes my Nan takes me there. She goes to the dentist because she has pretend teeth and the dentist gets to make new ones. He makes them with fire and things. Maybe they are hot in my Nan's mouth. When she got her new teeth she let me go to the sweet shop. Then I got sweets and ate them all up before we got home.

I go to the shop. I remember where it is because I am big now. I get crisps and a drink. But I don't look at them. I get very fast because the shop keeper is looking at me. Then she can see that I am a robber and I have stolen money. Maybe she will call the police and I will go to jail.

But the shop keeper doesn't ask me about the money. She lets me pay and gives me some more money back. I put that in the bottom of my school bag. I put it all in tissue because it bangs together and makes a noise. Then people will get to hear all the stolen money that is in there and I will have to give it back. Then I will be in trouble.

I eat the crisps and drink all up. They go very fast because I am very hungry inside. I wish I have more food. But I don't want to go to the shop because then maybe the police is there waiting for me. I go to play at the park. It is next to my school. Next to the big side called juniors. I am on the big side. I am a first year junior. I am seven. My classroom is at the back. It is millions of miles away from the big doors.

The park is all boring by myself. I play on the swings and on the slide. But there isn't anyone to play with. The slide is giant. Maybe it is bigger than a house. I get all the way up the steps and sit at the top of the slide in the house. There is no one there and I don't get told off for sitting at the top and not going down. Girls do that. They are scaredy cats because the slide is big. They get to be annoying because they just sit there and don't move. Sometimes I push them down and then they cry.

I get my book and I sit at the slide and read until all the mums and dads start to come. Then everyone is in the playground. It doesn't be time for school yet. But we are allowed to play in the playground until the bell rings. All the children get to play with footballs and skipping ropes.

Sometimes if she is early then I got to play with Kirsty before school. But she doesn't always get there on time. Not to play. Just for when the line starts. I don't get to play with Damien and Ben either because they are still in the other side of the school. They are third year infants. Next year they will get to play because then they will be in the juniors too.

I have a new friend though. His name is Peter. He sits at the table with me and Kirsty. They are both new to the school. But they don't come from the same place before. They just start on the same day and then they are my friends. Peter doesn't know lots of things though. My dad says he is brain damaged and that makes him slow in the head. But I like him. He doesn't pick on me.

The bell rings and we got to go to our classrooms. We all have to stand in a line. I stand with Peter and Kirsty and then we all stand in the long line. I have got there first so we are at the front and I have saved them a place. Then they get to be first too.

There is a boy that is mean in our class. His name is Mike. He is horrible to everyone. He asks me why my clothes are all dirty. I have got blood on my clothes and there is the yucky stuff from my dad. I didn't see it before. But it is there and I wish I could get it off.

"Maybe you need a bib like a baby," he says.

And then he calls me a baby lots of times. Lots of other children laugh. Peter tells him to shut up. But Mike doesn't. He says that I smell like wee and maybe I need a baby nappy too. I tell him to get lost and then I walk to the end of the line so he doesn't call me names again. Then people don't laugh.

# TELLING TEDDY

## TWENTY SIX

*I am so bad that the teacher doesn't let me go to school now. Maybe the sea can wash me all away and I don't have to go home again.*

I don't like it when the other kids keep saying bad things. They say them to each other. But I know it is about me. They ask what the smell is. They walk away so I don't make them scrunch their face up. It makes me feel sad. I don't be that bad. It is just my clothes.

They say it at the classroom. It makes me angry. I want to bash them and tell them to shut up. But they call me names. They are mean. But I don't be able to shout at them because the teacher will tell me off. I wish the teacher will tell them off. But I don't want to tell because my dad says when people tell on you it makes you a tell-tale.

Tell-tale-tit!
Your tongue shall be slit,
And all the dogs in the town
Shall have a little bit.

My dad sings it all the time when I tell on things. He sings it when I tell him to stop it with his finger. Because he keeps putting his finger in his mouth. Then he winks at me and it makes me feel all bad inside. I don't like it because then my dad knows about my badness and what it makes him do. If I say stop it too loud. He tells me I am a tell-tale and then he sings his song.

I don't want to be a tell-tale at school. Then the children won't like me anymore because no one likes a tell-tales my dad says.

I wish I can go somewhere and go to sleep. I am very sleepy. Then I can wake up at home time and no one will say anything bad to me. Because then I don't be there.

We have to all stand at the lunch line. I stand with Peter. There is a boy in front of me. I don't know who he is. He is from the bigger class. But he is talking to his friend. He asks his friend what the bad smell is. He makes me feel angry inside. No one will stop it. They all keep saying the smell words. I want to make them all go away and shut up forever. I push him. I do it my hardest. I tell him to shut up. I make it all loud like my dad does. My mouth wants to shout. I wish I am allowed to use the bad words like my dad.

The boy lands on the floor. He doesn't shout back at me. But he doesn't cry yet. The teacher has seen me do it. Not my teacher. It is one of the other ones. She tells me to get out of the line and get to the head teachers office.

Now.

I do. I make my arms cross over. I wish I could push the boy over again. Lots of the other kids look at me. I want to push them too. I wish I could make them all invisible. Maybe I can. Maybe me and Mr. Ted can write and make everyone go away forever.

The head teacher isn't in her office. It is all empty. But the teacher tells me to sit down and then she will go and get the head teacher. They don't like bullies at the school. I say I am not a bully. But she doesn't listen to me. No one listens to me. I am bad all the time.

It is the stupid boys fault. He said stupid words. Now I don't get any lunch too. I don't want to cry about it. But my tummy is very hungry inside. It hurts very bad. I don't have anything to eat at all. Maybe I will get to miss lunch time. And then I don't get seconds too. I want something to eat.

The head teacher comes in. She sits at her desk. She has stupid glasses on and she sits there and then she stares at me. She does the same stare thing my dad does. I don't uncross my arms. I get my angry face like my dad's. She doesn't shout at me. I think she is going to. But she doesn't say anything at all. Maybe she is ignoring me. Like we do to people in the class room when we don't like them anymore. I don't care if she doesn't like me. I don't care if no one likes me ever again in the whole world.

I want to make her not do the stare thing.

I don't like looking at her face. She has a big lump on the side of her head. My Nan says they are called moles. I don't know why they are called moles. Moles are things that live in the ground and look like little bears. But she has one of the lumpy things and it looks silly.

Someone knocks on the door. It is going to be the teacher with the boy. They will make me say I am sorry to him. But I am not sorry. He has to be sorry first. He said the stupid words first. He started it. I don't look at the door. I don't want to see the teacher or the boy.

The head teacher says it is okay to come in. I hear my dad's voice. It makes my tummy jump around inside. I wish I could cry. But I can't let my eyes do it. I stare at my feet. I don't want to look at my dad's angry face. He will do the stare thing too.

My dad sits on the chair. It is next to me. He doesn't touch me or hit me or anything. But I know that he will do it. I have been bad. I get hit when I am bad. When I get home he will hit me and lock me in the bedroom for the bad man.

The head teacher tells my dad about the boy that I had made fall over.

They ask me why and then they all look at me. I don't know why. I shrug my shoulders at them and keep my arms cross over.

The head teacher says that maybe it is better if I have a long weekend to calm down and think about the bad things I did. She says that she doesn't like bullies in her school.

"The way you have behaved today is unacceptable," she says. "We won't have children pushing other children over."

She says I am going to be something called suspended. It means that I don't go to school again until Monday. I am not allowed because I am bad. I have never been suspended before. I don't know anyone that has. I tell the head teacher I am sorry. But she doesn't listen. She says maybe if I am sorry then I will be good after Monday.

My dad has his car at the school. It isn't very far to walk. But my dad makes me get in the car with him. We get to the house I don't want to get out of the car. I look at the house. He is going to make me go to the bedroom. I don't want to. My tummy is all tired inside. I don't get anything to eat again because I am so bad. I don't ever want to go in the house again.

I get out of the car. My dad doesn't get out yet. I walk to the gate. But I don't go into the garden. I don't want to. I run away. I run my fastest. I don't look when I got over the road. I don't want my dad to catch me. He is lots bigger than me and he can run very fast. I run all the way to where the sea is. There are three bits of it and I run all the way down to the bottom.

I am not allowed to go on the beach part. The chain is up because the sea is nearly there. I sit on the wall that stops the sea coming and washing everyone away. The waves aren't very big. They splash at the bottom and I watch them. It is all hard rocks. With the green slippery stuff on them. I play there sometimes. But it hurt lots if the green stuff makes me slip.

I sit at the wall for a long time. I don't have anywhere to go. I wish I could close my eyes and go to sleep. My eyes are sleepy and it is dark time. Fishing people come at the dark time. But they don't get there yet.

My dad comes though. He shouts my name. He stands on the steps from the higher part. I stand up on the wall. I don't want to go home. He will start the shouting at me again. My dad stops walking. He put his hands up like I do when I don't want him to hit me. He tells me to come down off the wall. He says I might fall.

I tell my dad he is going to hit me. I start to cry because I want to go home. My dad says if I get down off the wall we can go home. Then I can get some dinner.

"I promise," he says.

He crosses his heart and hopes to die.

## TELLING TEDDY

### TWENTY SEVEN

*Mr. Ted. I was bad today. I ate and I didn't be allowed to.*

My dad keeps his promise just like he said. He lets me have some soup and bread and I get to eat it at the big table. I get a bath and I have my own water. I don't get the cold water that my brother has got to use first. I have lots of water and bubbles. I am allowed to sit and watch the television. But I don't know what I want to watch. I go to bed and no bad man comes. He doesn't. Not at all. And my dad read the books to me. But he doesn't do the hurt thing to me. Not for being bad. Just a little bit when he reads the book to me. I go to sleep. My dad says we are going out the next day because I don't have school. So then I can go with them and we are going to the lakes. I tell Mr. Ted that I am very excited.

I don't be allowed to take him with me. But I want to tell him all about it when I get home. I promise him I will draw a picture of it and then he will know what it looks like too. I tell him I will miss him and wish he got to come too.

My dad says we can only go if the weather is nice. Not if it is raining. He says the rains are very bad at the lakes and then there isn't any point in going because all we will do will sit in the car all day and that will be boring. There is a number that we have to call in the morning. He says if they say it is nice then we get to go. I can telephone them. I tell Mr. Ted that we have a special thing to do and then we have to wake early so we can do it and not miss it. Like lazy bones.

Mr. Ted has the paper with the telephone number on it. He is going to look after it and keep it safe. Then it doesn't get lost. We will do our special job and then my dad will see that I don't be bad all the time. I tell my dad thank you and then I give him a hug.

I get up and use the phone. We can go to the lakes. We are going for all the whole day time. My mum makes some sandwiches for lunch time and she puts them in a box with an ice thing that keeps them all fresh and cold. We have to go very early because my dad says it takes a long time to get there and he doesn't use the big roads because it makes my mum scared. So we have to use lots of little roads and that makes it take a long time.

My tummy is going to pop because I don't know how to wait until we get there. I wish I can make the car go very fast and then we can be there like superpowers. If I could fly like Superman maybe I can lift the whole car up and we can be there very fast; faster than anyone. But I don't and it is going too slow and feels like forever.

We get near to the place and there are lots of giant mountains. They are all green and on the top is white.

"It is snow," my dad says. "Because they are so high up they touch all the snow in the sky and then it falls onto them."

I wonder if they are bigger than a beanstalk. Maybe Jack can get there and the giant can get down.

I ask my dad what they are. He says they are called The Pennines and then sometimes people got to walk up them and there are lakes there. There are little mountains too. They don't have the snow on the top as much. Maybe the lakes got all frozen. Maybe Jack Frost lives there when it is all hot and he doesn't be able to make all the snow and ice at the houses.

I ask my dad if we can walk up them one day. He says yes. But we have to buy special walking shoes or our feet will get all sore. It is a long, long way and it will take us lots of time. I want to go and see the snow.

We got to the lake place. There are lots of cars there and we park by the toilet building. There is a little park too to play on. It is all made out of wood and I wish Mr. Ted is here because then we can make lots of adventures. I ask my dad if I can go and play. He says yes but I have to take my brother.

They have lots of things there to play on. There isn't a slide though. But it has swings and ropes and lots of things to climb on. There is a big thing that has ropes to get all the way up to the sky. My brother tries to do it but he is little and he doesn't be able to get his feet to do it because they keep falling in the gaps.

We finish playing at the park. We follow the path all the way down. It smells funny. But I like the smell. My dad says it is the water. My mum and dad are lied on a rug thing on the grass. They can see the lake and all the boats that go passed. People can play in the lake with lots of little boats that blow up and then they float on there. There is an island too at the other side. My dad says if we look there is a big black train that goes around it. It is old and has all the smoke come out of the top of it.

There are lots of trees too. If Mr. Ted was here he could have come then we could have hid in them and make places to play. We can live in the forest forever and be monster hunters and then no one will ever get us because we will be the bestest in the world. I ask my dad if I can go and play. I want to look if there is a den in there. I bet I get to be able to make one. My dad says yes. I don't have to take my brother. He gets to sit with my mum because he is all tired again and wants his baby bottle and his coat.

I go to play for a long time. It is lots of fun. I get to hide in the bushes and pretend I am lost on an island. Then I have to find my way home again because nobody knows where I am. It is a secret. My dad knows where I am though. He finds me.

"It is time for lunch and your mum is giving sandwiches and some chicken," he says. "What are you doing?"

I tell him about the den and that I found lots of things to play with. My dad hits me in the tummy his hardest and I don't be able to breathe. I fall on the ground. I try to cry. But there is no air in my mouth and it doesn't want to do it. I don't be able to talk too. I didn't know he was going to hit me.

My dad puts his hand on the back of my head and he pushes it down. He squashes it down onto the ground. Maybe he is going to make my nose go into my face and then I will look stupid with no nose on my face.

"When you get to your mum, you don't get to eat anything," he says. "You tell her that you aren't hungry."

She doesn't know about the badness at school. But he does and he hasn't told her because then she will get madder and I will be in the big trouble. He squashes my head very hard and puts his face next to mine on the mud. It makes me cry and I don't be able to move. He makes my neck hurt.

My dad lets go of my head. But he has my arm and says that I don't get to go to my mum until I clean myself up. There is mud and dirt on my clothes. I wipe my face and then I get the dirt off my top. I go to my mum. But I don't look at her. Then she doesn't see I have cried and she doesn't ask why. Then she will get mad about the badness at school and making my dad put my head in the dirt.

I sit on the grass and cross my legs like we have to do at school. My mum has some chicken and she puts it on a tissue. I say no thank you and tell her that I am not very hungry.

My dad sits down. He smacks me on the back of my head.

"You are very ungrateful. Your mother spent a long time making that food for you," he says. "We don't have a lot of money and then you just waste it all the time."

I tell my mum and dad I am sorry. I get the chicken and I eat it all up.

I ask my dad if I can go back and play in my den after lunch time. He says yes and I play there all day until it is time to go home again.

I nearly fall to sleep in the car. I am tired from all the playing. My brother is asleep. We get home again my dad tells me to get to the bedroom.

"Right now."

I don't know if I have to get on the box or if I have to get into bed. I don't do any. I stand at the corner and then I don't move. I don't pick up Mr. Ted. He is still in the bed. I will tell him later about the lakes. I don't want to tell him about the hitting part though. He will be sad that I don't be good like I promised.

My dad comes up the stairs. Then he comes in the bedroom. He asks me why I ate the chicken. I tell him that he said to eat it. My dad says he didn't. He tells me that I wasn't allowed any lunch but I had gone and eaten it when I knew I wasn't allowed to.

"You never do what you are told."

My dad hits me across the face. He asks me why I don't ever listen. I say I do. I tell him I really do. That he tells me my mum has spent lots of time making the food and that I should eat it. I cry because he won't listen to me and then he hits me again. He says he didn't say I should eat it and I am lying. He hits me lots of times. He doesn't stop. I put my hands up so he doesn't do it hard. But he does and then I am on the floor and try to make myself go away. But he just hits me. He is going to do it forever.

## TELLING TEDDY

## TWENTY EIGHT

*I got a new car today Mr. Ted. I got it off Graham. He took my picture.*

Sometimes, I think my mum is silly. She does lots of silly things. But I don't ask her why because then she gets mad about them. I tell Mr. Ted. He doesn't know either. So we just do as we are told all the time.

It is just after Christmas. We don't go back to school yet because it is still closed until we get to the New Year time. But my dad has gone back to work. My mum tells me to go upstairs and I do. She doesn't shout at me. And I don't do anything bad.

It is nearly bed time. But we haven't had dinner because my dad isn't home yet. My mum gives me my school uniform and tells me that I have to put it on. I don't have school. Not when it is nearly dark time. But I do it anyway.

She tells me that I have to sit on the bed and stare at the window. I don't be allowed to move. Not even turn around.

"You stay right there," she says.

My mum pulls the curtains closed. But it isn't dark time yet. Just a little bit. There is still sunshine outside. Maybe my mum has got all the days mixed up. Sometimes she gets lots of things mixed up. I get to help her when her brain tells her silly things. The silly things make her scared. But she doesn't look scared with these silly things.

My mum goes out the room. She closes the door. But she doesn't make it locked. I wish I can turn around and look. But I don't. My brain keeps telling me maybe the bad man is there. But I don't hear him. Maybe he is very clever at no noise and then he will get me and I won't know about it.

I can hear someone's feet on the stairs. It isn't my mum's or my dad's. But my dad is still at work and I don't hear his bike yet with the big engine that makes all the growl sounds. Someone knocks on the door and opens it. I turn around. It is a man. I don't know him. He has funny hair. It is all like silver. He is nice and he has a big smile. He knows my name and he says hello and asks if he can come in. I say yes.

He asks if he can sit on the bed too. I tell him he can. He tells me that his name is Graham. Then he asks me about school. He asks what I like to do there. I tell him that I like to read lots of books.

He asks me what my favourite book is and I tell him it is one call the BFG. It is about a big friendly giant. He says that he has read that one. I don't know anyone that has read it. He says it is one of his favourites too. He asks me about lots of books and I tell him about them all. My mouth wants to say lots of things about all my books.

Graham says he has lots of books and sometimes they make him laugh lots. I tell him they make me laugh too. I say sometimes they are sad and he says yes. Graham says that I have a very nice smile.

"It is like the biggest smile I have ever seen."

I can't keep it away. No one ever says I have a nice smile before. He says it makes my eyes all blue and that they get shiny.

Maybe they are like magic. Like Superman when his eyes get all funny colours. Then he can get lasers out of them and shoot the bad people. Maybe I can get my eyes to do that and I can use them to get away from the bad man. I don't tell Graham about the bad man. I am not allowed to talk about him to anyone or he will come and get me.

Graham tells me about his wife. She wishes she had a little boy. But she doesn't. She got sick and can't have any children. He asks me if he can take a picture to show her. Then he will tell her all about my reading because she likes to read too. She will think it is very good because I am only seven.

I let him take my picture. He tells me to sit up near the pillow and lean against the back. I do and I smile really big so he gets a nice picture to show to his wife. Then maybe she doesn't see I have badness inside.

Graham says that maybe I can take off my tie and my school jumper because boys in shirts look nice and not so boring. I say okay and he helps me to take them off. Then he takes some more pictures and tells me to smile lots. He has a big smile too. He says I do the pictures very nice and he couldn't wait to show them to his wife because she will think I am very nice too.

He gets the pictures all done. He comes and sits on the bed. He leans on the pillows with me. He has a bag of sweets. They are white chocolate mice. They have pink stuff in their tummies. He asks me if I want one. But I say no. I know I don't be allowed sweets. But he says my mum told him it is okay. So then I take one and eat it. It is very nice.

We talk about lots of things. About books the most. But lots of things too. All the fun things he likes to do. He asks me about what I like to do and I tell him all about my friends at school. He lies down on the bed and tells me to roll on my side. I get to face the window. He asks me more about stories and things. I tell him all about the library.

Graham puts his hand on my leg and then he hugs me a little. I am going to roll over, but he tells me not to. Then he gets his hand at the top of my pants and he opens them. I get my hand on his. I don't want him to open my pants. But he says it is okay. He says he promises he isn't going to hurt me.

He gets his hand inside my pants and put it on my thing. It makes my tummy feel all funny inside. I don't know what I am supposed to do. My eyes feel like maybe they will start to cry. I hold my breath. Then I hear his pants get open. Maybe he is going to do what the bad man and my dad do to me. Maybe he will do the hurt thing. I try to move on the bed. But he hugs me. He doesn't hurt me. He says he promises he won't. He whispers that it is okay and to lie still. Everything will be fine.

The bed shakes and his hand moves about in my pants. And he does it harder. But he doesn't hurt me like he promised he wouldn't. He takes his hand out of my pants and says thank you.

Graham gets off the bed. He gets his coat back on. Then he puts his hand into the pocket and pulls out a toy car.

"This is for you. You can keep it," he says.

He says bye and goes down the stairs. I have a new car.

# J D STOCKHOLM

## TWENTY NINE

*Mr. Ted, my badness got out today.*

I don't know if I will get in trouble for going downstairs. No one has told me and I don't know what to do. Maybe I have to wait for my mum. I don't know that too. Maybe she is going to leave me in the bedroom all day long. I don't remember if I have been bad. But maybe I was. I haven't had my medicine yet. So maybe the badness got out and I don't know about it.

I look out the window. But I don't open the curtains. Graham has a big giant silver car. It is all new and shiny. Not like the car I have in my hand. But like the ones on the television. I squash my nose on the glass. It is cold. But I watch Graham drive all the way down the road and then he is gone.

I don't get off the glass. My breath makes it all steamy and I get my finger and draw a face in it. My mum will be mad if she sees. She always gets the windows clean on her cleaning day. She cleans them with special stinky stuff.

Mr. Ted is on the bed. He is on the pillows where my brother gets to be when my dad does the hurt thing. He had to lie there too when Graham had lied on the bed with me. Maybe he thought I am all bad inside. I get him off the bed and hug him my hardest. He smells like Mr. Ted. He doesn't smell bad like me. I can feel my badness inside. It feels like a funny badness. It makes me want to cry. But I don't. I don't let the tears get out of my eyes because there isn't anything to cry about. Maybe my badness is sad.

I tell Mr. Ted about the car. I don't tell him why I have the car. But I show him it. He likes it. It is all nice and new. It is shiny like Graham's car. It has all the glass in it and is made of hard stuff and won't get broken.

Maybe I can show the people at school. Then they will see I get good toys too. Maybe they will want it and I won't let them because it is all mine. I put it in my pocket and then I stand with Mr. Ted at the window again. I wish I could get my eyes closed and never ever open them. Maybe I can sleep for a long time.

## TELLING TEDDY

My mum shouts me. She doesn't come upstairs. She stands at the bottom. She tells me to go downstairs. But she doesn't tell me to get my uniform off. So I don't. I have Mr. Ted with me. We stand at the door and look at the hallway. There isn't anyone there. But my brain has lots of pictures. Lots of the bad man. I don't like them. They fill with his face. He always is laughing at me with his stupid eyes.

I hear my mum shut the door of the back room. It makes a click and a pop that gets to be two sounds. I make them click in my brain. I get to hear them. Then I don't see the bad man because I get pictures of the door. I hear my dad's bike too. The big growl like a monster in the alleyway behind the house. I know it will be dinner time.

The stairs make lots of creaks when I walk down them. I don't ever be able to sneak on them. The bad man does. He is good at the sneaking. But I don't be able to do it. I walk at the side. The sides don't have the carpet on them. It's wood. But I have to make the carpet feel the same on both feet. I go down them slow. It all gets to be the same then no bad man will come. I always do everything right. Me and Mr. Ted have talked about it.

I get in the back room. I get the door closed. It has to make the sound and then my brain makes the noise feel like a scratch inside. Sometimes my brain gets itchy if things don't be right. That is when the bad man is reading my mind. So I have to make it right. My mum tells me I am slamming the door. But I don't. I just get the noise to be right. My mum tells me to get the table set for dinner. I just make it for three. Because my brother is sleeping with his baby bottle and he doesn't eat real food anyway. I wish I get to eat baby food. Then I will get hugs all the time too.

I sit at the table. Then my mum gives me my dinner. I am not very hungry. I wish I could get to sit with Mr. Ted and read our books. I don't want to look at my mum and dad. Maybe they will see the badness inside. I can feel the evilness in there. I want it to go away. I want to hide from it. Then I don't get bad. I know the bad man is looking at me. He can see the badness in my mind because he has superpowers. I wish I could get it all washed away.

I try to eat my dinner. But it is hard. I put one bit in my mouth and then I make it swallow. But I have to eat another bit because my brain likes to do everything the same. I have a stupid brain. I wish it will go away instead of me. Maybe it can shut up with all the stupid things it says and the pictures that are all bad. It makes me do all the stupid things.

I have to make everything be even. We learnt about the even and odd things at school. There are two of lots of things. They are called opposites. One on each side. But I don't like to make it even with my dinner. Because that makes it the number two. I don't like the number two because it is a bad number. Bad things happened. We live at number two. I like number three. That is a nice number. But it makes it all odd again and then I have to eat some more food. But that makes it number four and four is a very bad number. It is the worst number ever. All the bad things happen if I do anything four times.

I don't be able to eat five bits of food though. Because that is bad too. I have talked to Mr. Ted about it. We like the number six the best. It is a nice number. Bad things don't get to happen and when we say the number it get to make the scratchy bit in our throats. Six is good. I eat six bits of food.

My dad doesn't like when I get the numbers all loud. But my brain says I have to do it. Then I get to feel the numbers in my throat. Then they are all right and nothing can be bad because I have made them all loud. My dad tells me to stop doing it.

"You're going to drive me mad with that infernal racket," he says.

But I have to do it. If I don't then the bad man will come. Then maybe he will make it all hurt inside.

I try to make the noise quiet. Then my dad doesn't get mad about it. But he can still hear it.

"You know," he says. "I have a friend once who made all those stupid noises. They sent him away to the loony-bin because that's what he is."

I don't want to go to the loony-bin. I am not a loony. I have just got a stupid brain that makes me do lots of stupid things. If I just get the numbers right then the bad man will know when he reads my mind and hears it. I don't tell my dad about the bad man. He will come and get me. He will get his nails and make them scratch all down my back like he does sometimes when he is going to do the hurt thing. Then he will make it hurt really bad.

## TELLING TEDDY

I don't want to eat any more of my dinner. My eyes just want to cry and I have counted. My brain doesn't want to think about it all. I wish I am able to make the food be invisible. I don't be able to eat any more. I get my fork and then I move it around. But I don't want to put it in my mouth.

My dad is mad at me. He gets to sit and do the stare thing at me. I don't like it. I try not to look at him. But my eyes keep on wanting to. Then he gets his hand and makes it slam down big and loud on the table. It makes everything jump about. Even the plates and the knives and the forks all get to jump. My brother cries too because he has been to sleep.

My brother doesn't like it when my dad gets all mad. It makes him sad and sometimes he gets all scared about it. It is my fault because I don't be good ever. Because I am stupid and bad and they all wish that I would go away. Nothing ever works to make me better. Not even the sick from my tummy. Or all the stupid big fat people at the church. No one ever makes me be good.

My dad tells me to eat my dinner. But I don't want to. I shake my head at him. My dad doesn't listen. He keeps telling me to get it eaten or else there will be trouble. But I don't want to and he isn't going to make me eat his stupid stinky bad food. I tell him no. I get my knife and fork down on the table and I don't pick them up.

My dad gets them and he puts them at me. I get my hands on my legs. I get my nails on my skin and I make it all hurt. But I tell him I am not doing it. I get my head all shaking and say no, no, no at him.

My dad gets out of his chair. He gets out so fast that even the chair falls away. He gets to me and then he hits me in the face. I don't cry. He shouts at me lots of times.

I don't be able to stop it. The badness gets out and it makes me shout at him. I get out of my chair. But it doesn't fall on the floor. I shout my loudest. I tell him that I am not his friend. I tell him I don't want to eat my dinner because I hate it and it is stupid. I tell my dad that I hate him too and he is stupid. My badness gets all big inside my tummy. There doesn't be a way to make it all come out. I just shout.

I get all the bad words too. I say those lots and lots of times. I use all the ones my dad says. But I don't know what they are. They make him really mad at me. My mum doesn't know what it is.

"What's wrong with you?" She says.

I tell her that it isn't me. It is them. They are all bad and stupid and I wish they will be invisible and go away.

My dad gets my arm. He digs his fingers in and then he tries to make me go to the hallway. But I don't want to. I don't let it get hurt. I try to make my dad not hold me. He isn't strong enough and I make myself fall on the floor. But my dad is big and strong and he gets me up and out to the hallway. I get my feet on the wall. But my dad hits my legs and carries me upstairs.

I scream my loudest. I call him all the bad names that my badness tells me to say. I shout them so they are very loud. I want him to let me go. But he doesn't. He gets me to the bedroom and then he throws me in there and I land on the floor. My dad gets out. He gets the door locked. But I kick and bash it and tell him to come and get me out.

I bash it lots of times and I bash the floor with my feet. I don't stop. My badness wants to make my dad let me out again. I hear my mum come upstairs. She is putting my brother to bed. I shout at her to let me out. I shout so loud that it makes my throat sore. She tells my dad that he needs to sort me out.

My dad is upstairs too. He gets to the bedroom and then he opens the door. "Are you happy now?" He asks.

But he shouts it at me. I take in lots of breath and make my words all big at him. My dad gets his hand and hits me and tells me to not ever dare shout at him. I fall on the floor next to the bed.

My dad gets his belt off. He makes it get the snapping noise when he bangs it together. I say the bad words to my dad and then he hits the belt on my leg. I cry but the badness is still there and I cry and shout at him about the belt.

I don't stop all the bad words. My dad gets my arm. Then he picks me up and puts me onto the bed. He is bigger than me. I try to get away. I tell him to get off me. I am going to run away to the beach again and I will sleep there forever. It is dark time outside. My dad won't find me. I kick and I hit my dad. I try to bite his arm. But he gets one hand and squashes me down.

My dad gets my pants open and then he pulls them off. I don't want him to do the hurt thing. I try to get off the bed. But

## TELLING TEDDY

my dad is like Superman. I can't get out of his hands. He gets his own pants open too. Then he does the hurt thing and I don't get to stop him. He lies on me and I get squashed. I can't breathe because he pushes my head into the bed and I don't be about to shout. He makes it hurt lots like the bad man does. I try to get my scream out. But I can't. My dad tells me to shut up and then he makes it hurt more.

My dad gets off the bed. He doesn't lie on me and make me squashed. But all my badness is gone. My dad leaves the bedroom. I don't get off the bed. I don't hug Mr. Ted. I don't do anything. I lie there and don't move.

## THIRTY

*Mr. Ted. Do you think we could be pirates and go away down the plug hole?*

I don't move. Not at all. Not for a long, long time. I don't want to move. I wish I can close my eyes and go away. Maybe if I wish hard enough then I will. Maybe like they do in the story books. There is someone magic that comes and makes them go to somewhere that is far, far away. When all the people get their eyes closed and then they wake up somewhere else. Maybe I can do that and no one will ever find me.

I stare at Mr. Ted. Not the stare that my dad does. Mr. Ted isn't bad like me. I just stare at him. I don't know when he got there. Maybe he sneaked there when I didn't look. He lies there too and looks at me. His eyes don't move and he doesn't talk. Not out loud. Just to me because he is magic. He is my friend even when I am bad and call my dad bad names. It is a secret. Only I get to hear him. He talks inside my head.

Sometimes I think about Mr. Ted. I wonder what he does when I am asleep. Maybe it is all boring for him. I don't know. But he says it is okay. I hope he doesn't get sad when I am at school. Maybe the bad man comes and hurts him too. But Mr. Ted is never sad. He doesn't be scared of the bad man. Mr. Ted is good. He doesn't have the badness inside him.

My brother doesn't have badness too. That is why the bad man doesn't get him. My brother is nice. My mum says that he has to be treated gentle because he gets sad very easy. I don't like when my brother is sad.

My dad doesn't do the hurt thing to him. He doesn't get as bad as me. He is a good boy and I am the bad boy.

The badness makes everyone do hurt things to me. I just don't be able to get good.

I hear someone upstairs. I don't listen to their feet. Maybe it is the bad man. I don't look and I don't watch the door. I just get my eyes closed and maybe I can make it all go away. I feel my badness inside. Not like before. It doesn't want to shout. But it gets there. It is where my heart is. I don't be able to make it go away.

## TELLING TEDDY

It is my mum. She has been in the bathroom. She comes to the bedroom. But she doesn't come in. She stands at the door and tells me she has made me a bath and that I have to go and get in it. Then she leaves again. I don't answer her. I lie there and look at Mr. Ted. Maybe he looks at my mum. I don't know. She goes back downstairs then I hear her close the door downstairs.

It is all cold because I lie there with no pants on. My Nan always says that if I don't dress properly I will get a chill. Maybe Jack Frost will come and make me all cold inside and then I will get sick and can lie in the bed forever. I tell my brain to get up. But it doesn't want to listen. Maybe it is sleeping. It doesn't tell me about the pictures like it does when I get to be alone.

I watch Mr. Ted. He doesn't get up too. Maybe he is all tired inside. Maybe he has got hurt and I don't see. I put my hand to him. I don't reach all the way because it hurts inside to move lots. I touch him a little bit. On his spikey fur. He doesn't have lots any more. The bad man pulled it out when Mr. Ted stopped him from coming. But Mr. Ted doesn't be cold.

He doesn't make the noise from his tummy any more. My Nan says his squeaker is broken. Maybe that is why he doesn't talk out loud. Sometimes when I press his tummy he makes a little squeak. But I don't tell anyone about it. It is a secret that he can talk.

I tell my brain to make me get off the bed. It does. But it doesn't move a lot because it hurts inside very bad. I hold my tummy when I get off the bed. But I don't be able to stand up. My legs don't want to and when I try, my eyes cry. I stand on the floor and make myself into a ball. I put my head on the bed hug my tummy. I don't get any sick from it. It just hurts very bad. I wish I can get medicine to make it go away. But I don't tell my mum about it. She will be mad.

I don't let my cries get loud. Stupid boys don't cry. They don't get to because it is all their fault. It is my fault too. I made my dad all mad and then I made him do the hurt thing. I am not supposed to cry because I am bad. I don't want my mum and dad to hear me cry. They will think I am a baby. I don't like to be a baby. I just want the hurt parts to go away.

There is some blood on the floor. There is some on the bed too. I don't want my mum to see it. She will get mad that she has to clean up and it is dark time. I put the cover so she doesn't see it. She doesn't like cleaning things all the time.

"I never get to sit down and have five minutes to myself," she says.

I don't want her to not be able to sit down and then get sad about it.

I don't stand all the way up. It hurts lots when I try. I get myself like when I do the monster to my brother and I get him all scared. A hunch back monster. He is green and has lots of sharp teeth and then he eats little brothers. I walk like that. Like the big green monster.

The light is on in the hallway. I am glad. Then I don't have to be scared of the dark. There isn't anyone there. My brother is asleep in his bedroom. I can see the picture of the train on his wall from his light. He is very lucky that he has a nice room and lots of nice things. He is lucky he doesn't have the badness inside him like I do.

I hear the door at the bottom of the stairs. But I don't hear anyone come upstairs. It is my mum. She asks if I is in the bath yet. I say I am going to get in it now. She tells me to hurry up. They don't want to be waiting all night long.

I don't let her hear my cries. When I get my breath all held inside. Then I can say okay and she doesn't hear my stupid baby sounds.

My mum has let me have new water for the bath. Not like in the other days when I get to use my brother's. It is all clean and there is no dirty water in it. I don't get bubbles. My brother has bubbles. He gets a special bottle that looks like a pirate to make his bubbles. But it is all his and I am not allowed to use it. It is special just for him. I don't have one.

I get the rest of my clothes off. I try to make them in a nice neat pile. I have to fold them in a special way then my mum won't get mad because they don't get all creased up. I don't be allowed to put them on the floor. I put them on the chair. I get in the bath. But the hurt makes me not be able to breathe when I climb over the side. But I get in and try to sit down.

The water is warm. Not like when I get baths before and they are cold. I lie all the way down. It gets the water over my face. I lie there under the water with all the water on my face and I don't move. I get to listen to the water make swish noises in my head. The water gets in my ears. It presses hard and I get to feel it there. It tries to get out. It is in my nose too. The water gets all in my head and makes it all fill up.

I lie there a lot and don't get up. Maybe I can lie there forever and be like a fish. I don't put my head out of the water and get air. I can lie there forever and ever. I can hear my heart in the water. It is like when the nice doctor let me use his doctor thing and I got to listen. It bangs loud in my ears.

I can feel all the tired inside. My brain wants to go to sleep. I feel like I have gone invisible. Maybe I can go to somewhere else. Maybe I can float away in the water and down the drain. I can get to the sea and maybe the pirates will find me.

My heart gets all loud. I can't hear anything else. It is like banging. I let my eyes get closed and my brain wants to sleep. My arms and legs all float. I don't feel the hurt parts. Maybe I get the magic to work and I can live under the water.

I don't hear my dad get up the stairs. And I don't hear my dad get in the bathroom. He pulls my arm and he drags me up out of the water so I get to sit up. He makes my brain wake up. It has been really fast asleep. It feels like it has gone away. I don't know why he is there. I don't be bad. My badness is inside. It gets mad at my dad for getting me out of the water. It is nice in there. I don't want him to make me get up from it.

"You're not in the bath to lie there and pamper yourself," he says.

I don't say any words back. I don't know what words to say because maybe the bad ones will get out again. I look at him with my angry eyes like my mum and dad do. He tells me to get myself washed. He sits on my clothes on the chair and does the stare thing.

My dad tells me to let the water out then I have to get out of the bath and get dry. I do. But it hurts to climb out. I don't let my dad see it. I hold the sides of the bath and get my legs out slow. Then I get the towel from the rail at the wall.

My dad hits me with his belt. It hurts so bad. I can't hide the cries. I don't know my dad has his belt. I don't hear him with it. Not like before when he snapped it to make lots of noise. I don't know he is going to hit me. I don't know I have been lots of bad again. Maybe he can read my mind like the bad man does and that is why he does it. It makes me scream because I can't get the hurt to go away. It feels like he has pulled all the skin off. The belt hits my legs and bottom and I am all wet. It stings so bad I don't know what to do about it. I get my hands where he has hit me and I try to press it all away. But it won't go and I can't breathe because it hurt so bad.

My dad shouts at me. He tells me to get to the bedroom. He tells me to get dressed and sit on the box. I don't be allowed in the bed. I don't be allowed to even dare.

## TELLING TEDDY

### THIRTY ONE

*Mr. Ted. I have been very good. I sit on my box all night long and I don't ever let the badness out.*

Maybe if I sit in the corner for a long, long time and don't move at all I can get cobwebs on me. It will be like a spooky house when the skeleton sits in the corner and has all the dust and cobwebs and makes everyone scared. Because maybe there are ghosts. I like spooky places. they don't make me scared. Me and Mr. Ted draw lots of them in our book. I can be like a scary skeleton that has bones and sits and says boo lots of times.

My dad says that I have to sit on the box in the corner of the bedroom all the time. I don't get to move at all. Except when it makes my legs hurt. Then it feels like I am going to turn into a statue. Maybe when people get turned into statues they don't talk. Because their mouths are all glued together and they can't say help. I want to ask Mr. Ted if maybe statues are real people. Like when Medusa gets them with her snake hair. Maybe they go to sleep and things like that.

I am not a proper statue. I don't move lots. But sometimes I do and I watch the sun wake up and get its hat on. Then it goes back to bed and I wait until it gets up again. I do that lots of days. And I don't be a statue because I don't sit still when I am not at school. Just at the night time when I am bad and my mum and dad don't want to look at me.

I get to play with my cars when I sit on the box. Graham comes and sees me sometimes when I sit on the box and then I am allowed to get on the bed. Because he says it is okay. I lie there with him. He likes to take pictures. He says his wife thinks I am very nice. Maybe one day I can get to meet her.

My dad lets me lie on the bed too when it is time to read the stories to my brother. I lie on his arm with Mr. Ted and he does the hurt thing. But he doesn't do it like before because I don't be bad again or say bad words to him. I sit on the box like I am told and then I don't move. I don't be bad ever again.

I am good at balancing. I am not allowed to stay in bed when my dad has read the books. He gets out and puts my brother to bed and then I sit on the box and have to sit up. But I get tired and my eyes go to sleep when I don't know about it.

Then I don't move because I am good at the balance part and I don't fall over.

Mr. Ted sits on the box too and we write stories. I hug him lots of times when it is dark. We don't have any covers and it gets cold and maybe Mr. Ted will catch a chill because it is winter time outside and it is very cold. Even Jack Frost makes all the windows get icy. They have lots of icicles.

I go to school in the morning times; I like to walk at the park before the school gates get open and all the mums and dads come. Then I can walk on the grass and it is all frozen and crunchy when I stand on it.

It is nice when it is spring time. It isn't cold in the morning when I wait for all the mums and dads. Sometimes when it is winter time it gets too cold to sit on the slide and read. It makes all my teeth shake and bash together, but if I get on the swing instead then I can make it go high up to the sky and make me warm.

I know it is spring time now because my mum has a birthday. I am not allowed to be there. I am not allowed because I will be bad and make it sad like I always do. So me and Mr. Ted sit on the box. I always sit on the box after school. When my mum has made the badness be sick from my tummy with the medicine. On my mum's birthday she get lots of cards. But I go upstairs and just listen to them have lots of fun. Me and Mr. Ted made my mum a birthday card. We drew on it and made up a funny story inside it. But I am not going to give it to her. It is too stupid and she will get sad about it. Me and Mr. Ted put it in my chocolate tin and keep it safe in there.

I keep my cars in a box too. It is a box I got from my Nan. It is like the chocolate box. But it had biscuits inside it. If I put my face and smell the box I can smell all the biscuits. Maybe when I am good I can get something like that. It makes my tummy all hungry.

It is nice for my cars. I keep them all inside. I have fifteen cars. They are all new and I like them very much. I am going to keep them forever. Graham always gives me new cars. I wish I can pick some myself. Maybe he will get me one like the Nightrider car and it is all black with the red light at the front. I really wish I get one of those.

## TELLING TEDDY

### THIRTY TWO

*Mr. Ted. I got to see a strange lady today. She asked me about my badness, but I didn't tell her.*

My mum is at school. It is home time. She doesn't come to school anymore to get me. Maybe I have been bad and I don't know about it. But my mum doesn't shout at me. She says we have to go and see a lady at the school. I have to see her at the top room. It is a room at the top in a tower. Peter says that is where they keep people and maybe they chop their heads off. Then at night time the ghosts all walk around the school. I wish I got to see a ghost. Maybe we can sneak at the school one day and see if there are ghosts with no heads on them.

I ask my teacher about the ghosts with no heads. But she tells me off about that. She says I shouldn't think about dead things and I am not allowed to say it. Because I will get the other children scared that maybe there are ghosts when there isn't any really. She wrote it in my school books too. I draw lots of pictures. Mr. Ted says they are good. But my teacher doesn't like them. She says they are something called morbid.

Maybe my teacher doesn't like monsters and lots of dead things because she gets all scared. I don't be allowed to show my brother either. My mum says I make him all scared and then he will get nightmares too.

I go and see the lady with my mum and she asks me lots of questions. It is all about lots of stupid boring things. She gets some blocks and then she makes them into a house. I get told off for swinging on the chair and not looking at what she is making. But she is playing with baby toys and I don't want to. They are boring. My brother has baby things to do, not me. I am big.

The lady tells me that I have to make them all the same like she did. I don't know why she wants me to play with stupid baby toys. They are boring. It is a stupid thing to do. I make them all up like she says. I get all the colours right and all the same shapes. It isn't very hard to do. Maybe even my brother can do it and he doesn't know anything because he doesn't go to school.

She tells me to sit down and then she gets my school book. The one with all the pictures. It is the book we get to draw in. Mine has lots of pictures of the forest place. I draw all the pictures that my brain has about the bad people there. I draw the blood and the ugly faces. She asks me what it is and I shrug my shoulders because I don't know. But my brain does and when it tells me about them then me and Mr. Ted draw them all. I draw the house too where we live. But I put lots of dead people in there and the bad man's big bad yellow eyes.

The lady asks me about it. But I don't tell her. My mum does though. She tells the lady that I think there is a demon that gets to talk to me at night time. She tells her I see him upstairs when I go to bed and then I shout about it, but there is no one there. The lady ask me if that is true. But I don't want to tell her. I don't talk about the bad man. He will know and then he will make it hurt at the night time because I say bad things about him. I shake my head and don't tell the lady.

She asks me if that is why I get all the bad pictures. I tell her that it is the badness. She doesn't know what the badness is. I tell her that the devil tells me to do bad things and she asks if I can hear the devil talk to me. But I don't. He just makes me do all the bad things.

I ask my mum if we can go home. I don't like to talk about all the bad stuff and the bad man. Maybe he will get mad at me. It makes me feel the evil inside my tummy and then maybe all my sick will come out on the floor and I will get in trouble. Then my dad will do the hurt thing because my badness gets out and I don't mean to. I don't want my eyes to do the crying thing because I am bad and stupid.

I am happy when we get home. I go and sit on the box again.

# TELLING TEDDY

## THIRTY THREE

*Did you like the sleep over at Graham's house Mr. Ted? I did. It was so much fun. I want to do it again.*

Graham and my mum are sitting at the table. I don't ever see them talking before. I don't know that they are friends. Graham smiles at me. I like when he smiles at me. It makes me smile too because he is nice. Mr. Ted likes to smile. But he does it when it's a secret because no one can know that Mr. Ted is real.

My mum says Graham wants to know if I want to go out with him and I can get to sleep at his house too. Like a sleepover. I have never had one of those before. My friends do at school. They get to sleep at each other's houses. I tell my mum yes please and she tells me to take my school bag upstairs and then I can go.

I take Mr. Ted. He can stay in the house with me. Maybe he will like a sleep over too. But I don't want to get him all lost. My mum and Nan always say I don't be able to take him places with me. I tell him he has to be safe and I put him in my carrier bag. I get my tin with my book and my cars too. Then we can get to play and write about it. I am so excited in my tummy I don't be able to keep it away.

I forget to count. My brain tells me when I am going to leave the bedroom. I always have to count. It makes me feel funny inside. I say box and I make the X part scratch at my throat when I say it. But it doesn't make the feeling go away. I stand at the door and look. Maybe the bad man is going to be waiting because I didn't count the stairs when I went up them. I had forgotten. I am all excited inside. Stupid boy.

The wall at the stairs is all lumpy. That makes the numbers feeling go away. There is no bad man in the bedrooms. He isn't hiding. I get my hand on the wall and make my nails scratch all the way down and I count all the steps when I walk down them. I get my feet to stand at the sides so I feel the edge of the carpet in my shoes. It makes it all feel better and I go in the backroom and tell Graham that I am ready to go.

I sit in his car. He lets me sit in the front seat. I don't ever do that before. He says it is a long way and we stop where my dad gets petrol for things. He fills the car up and then we go inside the shop part and he asks me what I want. I don't know what I am allowed. My dad doesn't ever let me have things.

He asks me if I want something to drink. I don't know if I am allowed to say yes. I whisper it. I make the Coke word scratch at the C and the K part. Then maybe I don't get shouted at. He doesn't shout. He says okay and then he gets one and pays for it and gives it to me. I don't know if I am allowed to drink it.

We get back in the car. He says it is a long time to drive. But he talks to me about school and my stories and all the books I like to read. I tell him about the stories. He asks if I will read one to him. I don't ever do that. My mum always says they are stupid. He asks me and he uses the word please.

I get my book out of my tin and then I get Mr. Ted too. Maybe he will think it is okay to read the stories to Graham because he wrote them all too. We get to read one about Mr. and Mrs. Broom. But I don't get to read lots of it because Graham asks me about it and what they look like. He is silly I think. He thinks they are real brooms like brushes. I don't be able to read very well because I don't get the laughing to stop.

He makes my eyes cry because I laugh lots and I don't get all the story out. Maybe Mr. Ted will get mad because I don't read it properly. My tummy hurts, but not with the sick inside. I feel all the laughing in my tummy.

I ask Graham if his wife is going to be at the house. But he says she isn't. She has to work. But she is very sad that she can't get to meet me. He says he has a little dog though and the dog will be there. I don't be able to wait.

The house is so giant. I don't ever see a house like it before. Maybe Graham is rich. It isn't like our house. All the things look shiny. He shows me all of it and tells me that I can use the kitchen and bathroom any time I want to. He says he has lots of fizzy pop in the fridge too and if I want some I can just get it. He asks me if I am hungry and I say I am. He says he will make me some dinner and we can watch the television.

He has a box of Lego. He says he got it for me to play with after we eat some dinner. I get to sit and watch cartoons on the floor like my brother. But I don't get a baby bottle. I sit with Mr. Ted and we make cars and houses and lots of things. Graham is on the sofa and he has some work to do. It is lots of boring things about boring work.

## TELLING TEDDY

I want to go and get a drink. But I don't dare to ask him about it. I don't want him to shout at me. Me and Mr. Ted look at him and maybe he can get to read minds. Then he will get me a drink. He asks me if I am okay and I nod my head. I whisper that I am thirsty. He tells me I am allowed to go and get a drink. But I have to make sure I get the fridge door closed after.

Me and Mr. Ted sit and watch the television. Graham tells me that it is time to get a shower and go to bed. It is dark time. Me and Mr. Ted put all the Lego away all nice and tidy. He asks me if I wash my own hair or if my mum or dad do it. I tell him I don't be allowed to do it myself.

He has a bathroom in his bedroom. I don't know you can get bathrooms in bedrooms. Maybe then you get to sleep in the bath. He puts the shower on and makes it nice and warm and asks me if it is okay. I have never had a shower before. My mum has one. But it doesn't be the same as Graham's. Graham's get out of the wall. My mum has one that gets stuck on the taps.

Graham tells me to get undressed and get in the water. I do and he goes out of the bathroom. It is very nice to stand in it. I like the way it feels down on my back. I wish I can go to sleep in it. Graham knocks on the door and then he comes into the bathroom. He has got on a dressing gown. I turn around because he makes me jump.

He asks me what the mark is on the back of my leg. I forgot that I have got bad before. After the lady and my dad had hit me with his belt because I made my brother cry. I tell Graham that I don't know what it is. I don't want to tell him about the badness I have. Then he will make me go home again.

He gets my arm and then he turns me around. He gets his finger on it and he presses it. It hurts and I say ouch and move so he can't do it again.

"Did your father do this?" He asks me.

But I shake my head.

Graham makes me look at him. He does the stare thing like my dad and then he asks me again if it is my dad. I don't want to say it is. Then he will know about my badness. But I don't want my badness to make me a liar. Liars are bad. My Nan says so. I let my head do the nod and then Graham asks how. I tell him with his belt.

Maybe Graham is going to shout at me like my dad does. I am bad because I tell him. But he doesn't. He gets me into a hug. I don't ever have a big hug like that before. It feels all warm because he has his dressing gown on. He tells me that I am good and it isn't fair for my dad to hit me with a belt. I don't let my eyes cry. But they want to.

Graham has got his dressing gown all wet. He says that he might as well get in the shower too. He takes it off and puts it on the floor and gets in. He tells me to turn around so he can wash my hair. I do. He doesn't do it like my mum does. He doesn't make it all scratch and hurt my head. He does it nice and then maybe I can fall to sleep in the shower. All the bubbles go on my face. I wish I could stay here forever.

Graham says that if I don't get all the belt marks then maybe I can get to be an actor. He says I look all good and he knows I will be a good one because I will try my best. Then I can get to be in movies. He says he will talk to my mum about it if I want him to. I say yes please. But maybe my mum will get mad about it. But she likes watching the television. If I get to be on it maybe she will like me too.

Graham gets my hair all clean. He gets the soap and cleans me everywhere. Then he gets the biggest towel ever and gets me all dry with it. I don't have any pyjamas. I didn't remember to bring them with me. I don't want to sleep in my uniform. It is all stinky because I wore it all week. Graham says it is okay. I can just sleep like I am. It isn't cold at night time.

I get into his big bed. It is all giant and soft. I don't ever sleep in a bed like it before. Graham has a television too in his bedroom. He has lots of nice things. He gets in bed too. He gets his arm out for me to lie on it and I do. He gets his hands and he strokes my hair like my Nan does sometimes when I don't feel very well. My eyes close. I don't have to think about the bad man or anything. I fall to sleep.

I get waked up; it is lots of time later. Graham has his hand on me like he does at my house. But he doesn't do any hurt things. He hugs me and tells me to go back to sleep. I do. I sleep all night. When it is time to get up Graham gives me the biggest breakfast in the world. It has lots of bacon and eggs and bread and I have never had it before. I try to eat all of it. It is so nice. I get clothes too. My mum has given him clean clothes. I am sad that I have to go home again.

# J D STOCKHOLM

## THIRTY FOUR

*Mr. Ted. I got to go to Graham's house for all the weekend. I like it very much there. I hope he doesn't ever know I am very bad inside.*

I like when we get to stay at Graham's house and have the sleepovers. Me and Mr. Ted go lots of times. He likes it too. We get excited about it on Fridays because all my friends at school get sleepovers and I get one too. I don't tell them though. They get sleepovers at each other's houses. But I get a special one and I like it lots. Me and Mr. Ted get to play lots of games and we get to eat lots of things and Graham doesn't ever get mad at me. Not even when I don't stop all the talking. Maybe I am a chatterbox.

Me and Mr. Ted get to go every weekend. We go on the Fridays but not until after the school time and then I have to be home on Sunday because it is nearly school in the morning and I have to get bathed. My mum doesn't have to clean my uniform though because Graham does it. She likes that he does that because then she doesn't have to clean all the time.

I get to have pizza. I don't ever have one of those before. It is big and giant and I don't be able to eat it all up. Maybe I will make myself go pop and then I will get the pizza everywhere. It feels like I am going to. I eat lots of it and Graham keeps telling me I can have some more if I want to and it is so nice. I don't want to stop. But I don't be able to get any more in. The pizza is all the way down to my feet all inside until it gets to my neck. I don't want to be bad and get the sick out of my tummy. Graham doesn't ever shout at me if I don't eat all the food up. I got scared in my tummy the first time. It made my eyes nearly cry. Graham got to promise he wasn't mad about it.

We eat all the pizza and watch a film. Graham has boring work things to do. There is lots of boring things to read. They don't be very fun to talk about. Me and Mr. Ted lie on the sofa next to Graham and he reads his boring work things. I like it there and I watch the television with Mr. Ted. But I don't watch lots of it because I fall asleep and I don't know about it.

I wake up again I am lied on the sofa. But my clothes are all open. It isn't like when my dad does that. There is no hurt part. Graham just keeps his hand on me and then I squeeze up to him because I like it when he hugs me. He doesn't ever do the hurt thing because I don't get the badness at Graham's house.

Sometimes Graham gets his thing to touch mine. He gets his hands all in my hair and then he strokes my hair and I get sleepy and fall to sleep. He doesn't be mad about that either. He never gets mad at me.

I always get to sleep in Graham's bed. The bad man doesn't ever come. Not even in the bathroom. I always get showers and baths before me and Mr. Ted have to go to bed. Graham always gets to come in the bathroom. I like it when he makes me all clean again. But I get sad if he sees marks on me, like the things on my legs. But it is because of my badness and then my dad has to hit me because I don't ever behave.

I can feel the devil lots of times. He is inside and he makes my brain think about all the bad things. Sometimes I do them. I think the devil tries to make my evilness get my brother.

When he doesn't get so tired and I get to play outside. My mum says that he has to come out and play with me. I don't like when he plays with me. He is little and boring and he doesn't be able to do anything right. He makes me mad inside. I wish he would go away forever. Sometimes the devil gets the pictures in my brain about it. He shows me lots of pictures about making my brother go away forever.

I try it too. But I don't tell anyone. I don't even tell Mr. Ted. The devil just gets to be very good about things.

My mum made me take my brother to play at Phillip and Anne's or I wasn't allowed to go. We called for them. I rang the bell lots of times. But no one was home and so we had to go back to our house. My brother was bad. He didn't want to go home and I didn't be able to go home without him. He would have got lost and my mum would say I did it on purpose and then I would get into big trouble about it.

He was all mad when I tried to make him go home. He screamed really loud and I told him to shut up. But he didn't want to. He screamed lots and then he lied on the ground. I didn't be able to get him up properly. Because I had the hurt inside from my dad and it didn't let me move. But I picked him up a little bit and tried to get him home. My brother didn't want to go so he got his arms and legs all waving and then he made me drop him. He did it when we were in the middle of the road. I tried to make him get back up . But he didn't want to and he threw himself down.

I got my angry eyes at him just like my mum and my dad do. But he didn't want to listen. I said bad words and told him he was stupid because he was and he was going to get me in trouble. Then the devil got to give me the idea about leaving my brother in the road. Then I can get to watch the cars come and run him over. It would be his own fault. So I did. I got on the side of the road and then I watched him. I wished a car would be fast and come and then he could go away forever. The devil showed me all the pictures in my brain about my brother being squashed and all his blood and guts is on the ground. Like he went splat.

My brother just stayed on the road and then he started to cry about it. I don't like when he cries. It makes me feel sad inside. There weren't any cars. I got my brother again and gave him a hug and told him we have to go home. I said we could get to play Lego. I said please and then he standed up again.

We got inside the house. I didn't want to play the Lego. I got mad at my brother about it. Then my dad got all mad at me because I made my brother cry. My dad dragged me out of the room because I was bad. He hit me with his belt on my legs and then told me I get to stand in the hallway all the time. Because I am bad and he didn't want to hear about it.

I don't tell Graham that I got bad. But he sees the mark.

I don't want Graham to know I am bad. I like having a sleepover at his house. I like to hug all up to him. He lies in bed too with no clothes on. He hugs me very tight and we all fall to sleep.

# TELLING TEDDY

## THIRTY FIVE

*Mr. Ted. My mum and dad went away because I am bad.*

I don't ever see Graham again. My dad comes home from work. He says Graham has gone to heaven. I don't get to say goodbye to him. I close my eyes and maybe he can hear me when I say it.

I don't know why Graham has to go to heaven. Only old people get to go to heaven and he isn't very old. He doesn't get to say goodbye too. It makes my tummy hurt all inside when I think about him. I hug Mr. Ted and ask him why. But he doesn't know. He is all sad inside too because we like going to Graham's house. We try to ask my mum. But she doesn't want to hear about it. She tells me that I shouldn't ask about things like that. I can't stop the crying about it. I miss Graham. It hurts all bad in my tummy.

I don't know what she means. But I don't ask her about it anymore. I just don't know how to make it all go away from my brain. My brain wants to go there. I get to think about it on Friday and then he doesn't come to get me and I play with my friends. They get sleepovers at their houses. But I don't. Not ever again now Graham is all gone.

I do get my Nan home though. She has got better and the doctor says she can come back to the house. She still gets to go to the place in the day time. It is a place where people that are sad get to go. Then they get to be all happy because they get to do lots of nice things. Maybe I can go too and then I don't be sad about Graham. But my mum says it is just a place for stupid people like my Nan. My Nan doesn't be stupid. She is just sad.

I like my Nan living in the house again. I like she is there all the time. Then my badness doesn't get out all the time and she listens to my stories and things. Sometimes she is too tired and has to go to sleep. I don't make any noise when she is tired. I just wait for her to wake up again. At dark time my mum and dad go out. They go to the church place. Then they talk to Gaga and lots of other dead people. Maybe they get to talk to Graham. Maybe they can tell him that I miss him lots and lots and it makes my tummy hurt.

# J D STOCKHOLM

Me and Mr. Ted watch the television with my Nan. She watches something about cowboys. Me and Mr. Ted like it. But we try to be quiet and then maybe my Nan forgets we are there and she won't send us to bed. I don't like to go to bed all alone. What if the bad man comes and then makes my Nan fall to sleep or he gets to hurt her too? But he doesn't come. I listen really hard then he can't sneak up on us. I ask Mr. Ted to listen to and he doesn't hear anything. No bad man comes.

It is really dark time and my mum and dad don't be home yet. My brother is out too. He gets to stay up very late. Maybe he gets to sleep in the car or they have gone far away. I don't want to ask my Nan because then she will say it is my bed time too. But the cowboy thing finishes she turns off the television and tells me it is bed time for us both.

I don't want to sleep in the bed all by myself. Maybe the bad man will get in because my Nan gets to sleep and she don't hear anything. I don't know if I get allowed to sleep in the bed. My dad didn't say. He doesn't like when I sleep in it. He drags me out of the bed with my arms even if I am still asleep. Then he throws me at the box and tells me to not be so greedy and not to make any cry sounds. I don't be greedy. I don't know what I am supposed to do.

It makes me all scared in my tummy when my dad gets me out of the bed. Because I always think it is the bad man. He gets to make me jump like that and scares me lots. But then if it is the bad man I will go back to sleep again.

My Nan doesn't make me sleep on the box though. She lets me sleep in the bed and then she sleeps in there too. Maybe she gets to read my mind and knows that I am scared inside about the bad man. I close my eyes and get right to sleep.

In the morning time my mum and dad still don't be home. I don't know where they have gone. I don't even know they are going to go out. They have just not been there when I have got home from school. My Nan says it is okay. She says they have called on the telephone when I was asleep and said they are having a sleepover. I say okay and then I go to school.

Maybe I am too bad. Maybe the medicine doesn't work anymore to get my evilness gone. Maybe my mum has just had enough of me. She always says she has more than enough of my behaviour and she doesn't know why she ever has children.

Because we are nothing but trouble all the time. Maybe she wishes I get to go away forever.

I get home from school. I have been good all day long. I don't get told off by the teachers. I don't hurt the other children even when my brain tells me to do it. I just get to play with Kirsty and Peter. We play made up games about being lost. Then we get to swim in the shark water near the witch's house. I like making all the pretend stories with them. They like to play them too. We always have lots of fun. When I get to be going home time I think about it and I am going to tell Mr. Ted. Then we can write the stories and make new ones.

My mum and dad are home. They are outside. They have lots of things in their car.

It is a nice sunny day. It is after the Easter time when it gets to be all exciting that it is going to be summer time soon. My mum stands at the front door. She is smoking a cigarette. My dad is at the car getting lots of things in the back and my brother is in the car with his baby bottle and his coat. My brother has got to sleep in his seat.

My mum says they are going to be going soon. I ask where she is going because I don't know they have lots of trips somewhere. She says that they have got a new house to live in and it is all big and nice. It has a garden and is in somewhere called Hambilton which is a long way away. She says it is over the big bridge where the river is. It has trees and cows and farms. It is a nice place for my brother she says. Then he can have a garden to play in and have lots of fun.

My dad closes the back of the car and he smokes a cigarette too. He stares at me with that stare. Maybe I have been bad and I don't notice it again. That happens lots of times. I try asking Mr. Ted about it but he doesn't know. It makes my neck hurt to look at my dad because he is big. The sun is behind him and it shines in my eyes and makes me not able to see him properly. He says I don't get to go to the new house.

"You have school here," he says. "It will be too much hard work for you to get all the way to school."

Maybe I can get a new school. But my dad says there don't be any nice ones there near the new house. He shakes his head and says they is all full of bullies and I won't like them. He says that I have get lots of friends at my school and it isn't fair to move me away from all of that. I have to be a good boy for my Nan.

I don't want them to go. I want to go too. I don't want to stay here. I want to see the new house and get all excited about it. There will be no one when the bad man comes. I don't want to get all by myself when it is dark time. I tell my dad please. I say I will go to the new school and I don't mind if they pick on me. I will be good. I won't make any of the teachers be mad at me.

My dad says no. Then he walks away and I get his hand and ask him please. He says I am making a scene. But I don't. I want to go with them and not get left all alone. It makes me all squeeze tight where I get to breathe and where my heart is and I don't want him to go away. Maybe I don't get to see them again ever. I am sorry I am so bad all the time. My dad gets in the car.

I wish I have Mr. Ted. I get my hand inside my jumper and then I make it dig in  my arm so that the badness doesn't come out of my mouth. I ask my mum if I can please go with them. She shakes her head and then she goes to the car. I don't be able to stop my eyes from crying. I don't get to make it quiet. All my crying wants to come out all big at the same time. I get my arms on my mum and hug them around her so she get to make all the badness inside go away. I want her to see that I don't be bad and I want to go too and I am sorry.

I don't like the badness I feel inside. It makes me cry. It makes my heart all squash up and hurt. Maybe someone got inside and squeezes everything. I want my mum to hug me and take me with them. I don't be able to breathe properly and then my tummy hurts all inside. It all wants to be sick. My head wants to hurt too because I don't be able to get all the crying out and I don't be able to talk properly. Then my mum doesn't know what I am saying because all I do is cry like a big baby.

My mum shakes her head and tells me to stop it. She pulls my arms off her so I don't hug her anymore. I get my arms to hug myself because I feel all bad inside and it doesn't ever want to go away. I tell her to please don't go away. But she says it is too late they have already arranged it.

"If we had known you would have wanted to come with us we would have made plans for it," she says. "But we didn't think you liked being with us, so you have to stay here."

## TELLING TEDDY

My mum walks away and gets in the car. I tell her in my brain to please don't go. I say it lots of times. I close my eyes tight. Then maybe it gets to be real and she doesn't go away and they stay and come back for me. Maybe they will like me and want me to go with them. Maybe I don't be so bad all the time.

I squeeze my arms around myself to make it all go away.

"Please don't go," I say, lots of times so my mum knows that I don't want her to go.

My mum doesn't look at me. She doesn't get to see my words. Then my mum and dad drive away.

I try to run my fastest. I run as fast as I can. I run all the way down the road but they are in the car. It is all fast and they get to the end of the road before me. I nearly catch it when they stop at the end of the road. But then they drive away again and they don't see me. Maybe if they saw me they will stop and take me with them. But they don't and they are gone.

And they don't take me.

I get to the corner and the car is all gone away. I didn't be able to stop it. I cry and tell my mum to please come back.

"Just come back."

I can't breathe and my legs don't want to stand up. I sit on the ground on the kerb and then I make myself in a ball. I ask God to please make my mum come back. I will be good. I promise. If he just makes her come back. I won't be a bad boy again. I squeeze my knees to my tummy and I hug them really hard. I get my nails in my arms to make it all go away. My cries all get so hard that my head wants to hurt and the tears keep coming out. I cry on my legs so no one get to see.

"Please come back."

# J D STOCKHOLM

Feel free to contact me at any of these.

dearmrted@gmail.com

http://jdstockholm.com/

http://www.facebook.com/dearmrted

These two sites have been invaluable to me throughout the last few years. I salute the many people on there, survivors, directors and above all, my friends. Thank you for the support at those times I needed it.

http://www.isurvive.org.uk

http://www.recoveryourlife.com/

Printed in Great Britain
by Amazon